MIXSHAKESTIR

" Cocktails are a lot like food when it comes to flavor. A really great cocktail doesn't need a lot of ingredients, just a combination of tastes that balances the drink. It's often a single small element that makes the whole drink come together. Don't be afraid to experiment! "

BLUE SMOKE BARTENDER

MIXSHAKESTIR

photography   Jim Franco

food styling   Jamie Kimm

styling   Lauren Hunter

GOLD ST.
PRESS

07 introduction

17 favorite classics

Timeless, trend-resistant, and always exquisite, these cocktails have enduring appeal, a loyal following, and a memorable story.

115 elegant sips

Distinctive ingredients, pure flavors, unique pairings, and stylish presentations make these cocktails gorgeous and sophisticated.

149 casual libations

From a batch cocktail to serve a crowd to a savvy sipper for the beach or backyard, these spirited drinks deliver bright flavors and a carefree sensibility.

43 new classics

Whether it's the introduction of an unexpected ingredient, a twist on a flavor, or a finessed technique, these are fresh interpretations of old standards.

79 inspired flavors

Surprising combinations of ingredients, selected for maximum impact, deliver brand-new tastes in this lineup of innovative cocktails.

185 bar fare

Delicious party snacks, from salty nuts and chips to seasonal crostini, these favorites from the restaurants' kitchens satisfy every palate and accompany any libation.

214 recipes & reference

I can close my eyes and almost smell the ritual of "cocktail hour" in the St. Louis neighborhood where I grew up back in the 1960s and 1970s. My parents and their friends would take turns inviting one another into their respective homes for an open bar accompanied with Planters peanuts, sausage "beer sticks," and on special occasions, Boursin cheese and Triscuits. Wine was just about out of the question, although occasionally there would be a screw-top bottle of Soave or Chablis available for guests. Mostly people asked for the standards: Dewar's on the rocks, vodka Gibson, gin and tonic, Bloody Mary, and for the more adventurous, a bloody bull made with Campbell's beef bouillon. And then there were the nights my iconoclastic dad would drink his Pernod mixed with water (which seemed like a chemistry experiment gone very wrong), a vodka Negroni, or his all-time favorite, a glass of chilled white port. As for the smells—what I remember most was a lot of cigarette smoke, stale lemon rinds, and really cheap pickled onions.

I avoided cocktails for years. When I was in college, it was all about wine. In fact, I paid such scant attention to cocktails when I first opened Union Square Cafe, that our early guests chided me for creating an unwelcoming venue for real drinkers—devoid as it was of any liquor bottles on the back bar. Fortunately for me, and for the thousands of guests who have enjoyed our restaurants over the years, I became a convert to cocktails. And today's offerings have evolved by eons from those my parents drank.

Most of the credit for my own cocktail conversion goes to the extraordinarily talented bartenders, bar managers—and even cooks—I've had the privilege of working with, who have unleashed their culinary creativity to delicious results. Bartenders are increasingly taking cues from our chefs, who in turn are more aware than ever of how our beverages act as a condiment for the dishes they prepare. These are exciting times.

I am so grateful to my gifted restaurant colleagues who not only concocted, tested, and wrote the delicious recipes in this book, but who also contributed the many comments and tips for making great cocktails sprinkled throughout these pages.

Have fun with this book, and please come see us soon at any of our restaurants and bars!

Cheers,

Danny Meyer

inspiration from the kitchen

Great cocktails, like great food, spring from high-quality ingredients, inspired flavor combinations, and honed techniques. Cocktails have come a long way from the days of sour mix and Rose's lime juice. At Gramercy Tavern and its sister restaurants, drinks grow organically from the same sensibility of freshness, seasonality, and classic techniques that drives the kitchen—and applying those same principles at home can transform your bar.

seasonal ingredients   Let the freshest produce at the market guide your cocktail offerings. Choosing the best, just as you do for cooking, helps to ensure the perfect sip. Try muddling tiny Lady apples for a sweet-tart Smashing Lady (page 108), infusing pineapple juice with lemongrass for a refreshing Tablatini (page 100), or crushing pleasantly sour kumquats for a wintry mojito (page 162).

techniques   From knife skills to caramelizing, the tools and techniques you already employ in the kitchen can be put to work in your home bar. These concepts translate to garnishes and presentations, ingredients and flavor combinations: try thinly slicing the center section of a Bosc pear for a graceful garnish or charring sugared lemon slices with a kitchen torch to add the distinctive texture and flavor of a crème brûlée crust. Draw on the herbed vinaigrettes, fruit syrups, and flavored sugars of your culinary repertoire as inspiration for infused spirits, simple syrups, and rimming mixtures for your cocktails.

flourishes   Garnishes on drinks, as on dinner plates, are more than just stylish. They are an opportunity to layer flavors, highlight a specific element, or enhance overall appeal. They also give you the chance to be creative and add your own signature touch. A classic citrus twist contributes fragrant oils when squeezed into a drink, while a glass rim dusted with a spiced salt or citrus sugar adds a hit of savory or sweet flavor. A skewer of liquor-infused berries or a wedge of grilled watermelon also adds a colorful culinary flair.

> 66 With cocktails, the best investment can be a $3 bag of ice. Use it for mixing and chilling, then use your home ice to fill the glasses. 99

UNION SQUARE CAFE BARTENDER

ice

Whether on the rocks, shaken, stirred, or blended, cocktails are influenced by ice. This single element is so critical to good cocktails that Gramercy Tavern and Eleven Madison Park have a friendly rivalry over which restaurant has the best ice cubes. Here are some tips for the home bartender.

temperature Ice tempers the warming sensation created by the high-alcohol content of spirits. An ice-cold drink is a well-balanced cocktail.

freshness Ice cubes quickly pick up flavors from the freezer, so don't let them linger there too long. Use purified water and stainless-steel or silicon trays for the best-tasting (and clearest) cubes.

size Some cocktails show best with large cubes; others pair well with crushed ice. The size you use affects the taste of the drink and depends on the desired result. Larger cubes melt more slowly, preserving the flavors of the cocktail longer. Crushed ice melts quickly but guarantees a frosty glass. To crush ice without a crusher, wrap large cubes in a kitchen towel and break them up with a kitchen mallet.

dressed up For decorative cubes, place organic elements such as berries, melon balls, citrus zest, edible flowers, or herbs in ice cube trays, fill with water, and freeze.

" A garnish should have pertinence, adding another layer of flavor to a cocktail. "

THE MODERN BARTENDER

garnishes

Classic or creative, garnishes impart flavor and visual appeal to cocktails. Always choose a garnish that reflects the character of the drink and adds something to the composition, and use the best-quality, freshest ingredients available.

citrus Twists or wheels (crosswise slices) of orange, lemon, lime, or other citrus lend a decorative touch and essential oil flavor to any drink. Wedges are typically muddled when preparing a drink but also serve as an ideal garnish that adds additional citrus flavor. To make a twist, use a pairing knife, channel knife, or vegetable peeler to cut a long strip of zest from the fruit.

fruit & flowers These elements add color and flavor and can also give a drink a seasonal profile, such as strawberries in summer or candied ginger in winter. "Drunken" fruits, like brandied cherries, impart elegance.

vegetables & herbs Cooling cucumber, piney-sweet rosemary, crunchy celery, aromatic lemongrass—all add flavor, texture, and/or fragrance to a cocktail.

green olives Stuffed with everything from blue cheese to almonds, or even soaked in vermouth, olives impart a distinct flavor. A plain green olive, such as the Spanish Queen, remains a favorite for martinis.

13

INTRODUCTION

bar tools

 juicer Essential for preparing drinks made with fresh citrus. A handheld or manual juicer works well for lemons and limes, while an electric juicer is preferable for larger fruits, such as oranges or grapefruits.

 jigger A two-sided device for accurate measuring. The most common jiggers feature a 1-ounce cup on one side and a ½-ounce cup on the other, but it is useful to have a variety of jiggers in different volume measurements.

muddler An indispensable device for crushing fruits, herbs, and sugar cubes. A good muddler should be solid wood, have a large, flat head, and be long enough to easily clear the edge of a glass.

bar spoon A long spoon, usually spiraled down the length of the handle, used to stir drinks in a pitcher or shaker. Also known as a cocktail or mixing spoon.

shaker The cobbler shaker (left) contains a built-in strainer and a snug-fitting top. The Boston shaker, preferred by most bartenders, consists of a pint glass and a metal canister. The ingredients are added to the pint glass, then the metal canister is placed firmly on top to create a seal for shaking. The drink is strained from the metal canister.

 strainer The Hawthorn strainer (left) has coiled springs around its edges to ensure a snug fit on the metal canister of a Boston shaker. The julep strainer, which has a round, perforated bowl, works well on a pint glass.

glassware

martini glass Perfect for any drink served "up" (chilled then strained). To chill a glass, place it in the freezer for at least one hour; if time or space is limited, fill the glass with ice and cold water and let sit for several minutes, then pour out the contents just before using.

rocks glass This short, stocky glass, also known as an old-fashioned glass, is used primarily for drinks served "on the rocks" (over ice).

highball glass This tall glass helps keep bubbles intact, making it perfect for any cocktail with a carbonated component that is served over ice.

collins glass Similar to a highball glass but taller and narrower, this glass is named for the classic Tom Collins cocktail but is well suited for a variety of mixed drinks, especially when a frosted glass is desired.

champagne flute The tall, slender bowl of this stemmed glass showcases and preserves the effervescence of any sparkling drink.

wine glass The shape and size varies with the type of wine meant to be served in it. White-wine glasses, which are typically narrower than red-wine glasses, are used for a variety of cocktails.

hot toddy glass A durable glass cup with a handle, used for serving hot drinks.

favorite classics

A true classic has resisted trends to remain timeless. It has transcended generations and garnered recognition for its historical or cultural association and its combination of ingredients. It is a standard-bearer with enduring appeal.

Of the many classic cocktails, these are among the favorites of the bartenders at Danny Meyer's restaurants, each one selected for its inspiration, taste, and classic technique.

contents

❝ If you want to mix drinks like a pro, use a jigger. Measuring isn't stingy. It ensures proper proportions, which guarantees your drinks will be balanced and consistent. **❞**

TABLA BARTENDER

sazerac

Not surprisingly, this traditional New Orleans cocktail is a hit on Jazz Standard's cocktail list. Peychaud's bitters is essential to it—as is a soundtrack with some soul.

Pour the Pernod into an empty chilled rocks glass. Tilt the glass to coat the inside and pour out any excess. Fill a mixing glass with ice and add the sugar, rye, and bitters. Stir and strain into the coated glass. Garnish with the lemon twist and serve.

Splash of Pernod or other anise liqueur

Ice

1 teaspoon sugar

1½ oz rye whiskey, preferably Old Overholt

2 dashes of Peychaud's bitters

1 lemon twist

MAKES 1 DRINK

jack rose

Ice

2 oz applejack or
other apple brandy

¾ oz grenadine, homemade
(page 214) or purchased

1 oz fresh lime juice

1 thin apple slice or wedge

MAKES 1 DRINKK

The reputed gangster namesake of this applejack-grenadine cocktail may be why the pink drink, a seasonal offering at Eleven Madison Park, was a favorite of tough guys Bogart and Hemingway.

Fill a cocktail shaker with ice. Add the applejack, grenadine, and lime juice and shake vigorously. Strain into a chilled martini glass, garnish with the apple slice, and serve.

brandy crusta

1 lemon wedge and sugar for rim

1 lemon peel spiral, ½-inch wide

Ice

1½ oz brandy

¼ oz Cointreau or other
orange liqueur

¼ oz maraschino liqueur

¼ oz fresh lemon juice

MAKES 1 DRINK

Hailing from nineteenth-century New Orleans, this sweet-and-tart brandy-lemon sipper inspired a whole family of cocktails, including the famed Sidecar.

Moisten the outside edge of a chilled martini glass with the lemon wedge. Sprinkle a little sugar on a small plate and dip the moistened rim in the sugar to coat it lightly, then wrap the lemon spiral around the inside rim. Fill a cocktail shaker with ice. Add the brandy, Cointreau, maraschino liqueur, and lemon juice and shake vigorously. Strain into the prepared glass and serve.

applejack rabbit

This autumnal Gramercy Tavern drink combines Laird's bonded apple brandy—made in New Jersey by a distillery licensed in 1780—with Union Square Greenmarket apples and New York state maple syrup.

In a small pitcher, combine the apple brandy and maple syrup and stir until combined. Fill a cocktail shaker with ice. Add the brandy-syrup mixture and the orange and lemon juices and shake vigorously. Strain into a chilled martini glass, garnish with the apple slice, and serve.

2 oz apple brandy, preferably Laird's

$2/3$ oz pure maple syrup

Ice

¾ oz fresh orange juice

¾ oz fresh lemon juice

1 thin slice fresh or dried apple

MAKES 1 DRINK

old-fashioned

The origins of this classic, fruit-spiked cocktail are debated, as are its precise components, but Blue Smoke's version with Maker's Mark gives the nod to Kentucky.

Fill a rocks glass with ice. Muddle the orange wheel, lemon wedge, 1 of the cherries, and the sugar in a cocktail shaker until the fruit is broken up. Add ice to the shaker and then the bourbon and bitters and shake vigorously. Strain into the glass, garnish with the remaining cherry and the orange twist, and serve.

Ice

1 orange wheel, plus 1 orange twist for garnish

1 lemon wedge

2 maraschino cherries

1 tablespoon sugar

2 oz bourbon, preferably Maker's Mark

Dash of Angostura bitters

MAKES 1 DRINK

pink lady

Ice

2 oz gin

1 oz grenadine, homemade
(page 214) or purchased

¾ oz fresh lemon juice

Splash of apricot brandy

Splash of applejack or
other apple brandy

1 large egg white

MAKES 1 DRINK

A femme fatale favorite in the 1940s and still popular with Eleven Madison Park's female guests, this classic cocktail's elegant presentation belies the wallop it packs.

Fill a cocktail shaker with ice. Add the gin, grenadine, lemon juice, apricot brandy, applejack, and egg white and shake vigorously until frothy, about 30 seconds. Strain into a wine glass or pewter cup and serve.

bronx cocktail

Ice

1½ oz gin

½ oz sweet vermouth

½ oz dry vermouth

1½ oz fresh orange juice

Dash of orange bitters

1 orange twist

MAKES 1 DRINK

Famed Waldorf-Astoria bartender Johnnie Solon invented this gin-and-vermouth concoction before Prohibition. Nowadays, it's a rotating classic at Eleven Madison Park.

Fill a cocktail shaker with ice. Add the gin, vermouths, orange juice, and bitters and shake vigorously. Strain into a chilled martini glass, garnish with the orange twist, and serve.

3½ oz Prosecco, chilled

Splash of Aperol, about 1½ oz

1 sugar cube

MAKES 1 DRINK

venetian spritz

Union Square Cafe's version of a Champagne cocktail blends Prosecco, Aperol (an Italian bitter-orange aperitif in the Campari family), and a sugar cube, which is added at the last moment to set off a celebratory fizz.

Fill a flute three-fourths full with Prosecco. Add the Aperol; the color should be an orangey red, and there should be enough room in the flute for the drink to bubble up when the sugar cube is added. Add the sugar cube and serve.

> " Our cocktail menu features classic American drinks with an Italian twist. The Venetian Spritz is one of my favorites. Lots of people aren't familiar with Aperol, which has a bittersweet taste and a gorgeous rosy color, so it's nice to introduce our guests to a new flavor. "
>
> UNION SQUARE CAFE BARTENDER

ritz cocktail

The soignée Ritz evokes the Champagne cocktails sipped in Gilded Age grand hotels, when Eleven Madison Park's neighborhood was the center of New York City glamour.

Fill a cocktail shaker with ice. Add the Cognac, lemon juice, Cointreau, and maraschino liqueur and shake vigorously. Strain into a flute. Top with the Champagne, garnish with the lemon twist, and serve.

Ice

1½ oz Cognac

½ oz fresh lemon juice

½ oz Cointreau or other orange liqueur

½ oz maraschino liqueur

2 oz Champagne, chilled

1 lemon twist

MAKES 1 DRINK

FAVORITE CLASSICS

moon walk

Invented at London's Savoy Hotel in 1969 to honor the first lunar landing, this celebratory cocktail is a blend of bubbly, a double dose of citrus, and a subtle aroma of rose.

Combine the grapefruit juice, Grand Marnier, rose water, and Champagne in a flute and serve.

1 oz fresh grapefruit juice

1 oz Grand Marnier or other orange liqueur

Dash of rose water

3½ oz Champagne, chilled

MAKES 1 DRINK

Ice

1½ oz Campari

1½ oz sweet vermouth, preferably
Carpano Antica Formula

Soda water to taste

1 orange twist

MAKES 1 DRINK

americano

This Campari-vermouth blend was originally called a
Milano-Torino, after the cities where the two aperitifs
were invented. But American tourists became such big
fans of the cocktail that the Italians changed its name.

Fill a highball glass with ice. Add the Campari and vermouth. Top with soda
water, garnish with the orange twist, and serve.

" The Negroni hews to the classical. In our version, we use Punt e Mes, the bitter version of vermouth, which makes the cocktail more distinctive and savory—and a fantastic aperitif for sipping before nearly any meal. **"**

UNION SQUARE CAFE BARTENDER

negroni

Edgy and strong, this Italian classic—reputedly created when a Florentine asked a bartender to add gin to his favorite Americano—is popular at Union Square Cafe.

Fill a rocks glass with ice. Add the Punt e Mes, Campari, and gin and stir gently. Garnish with the orange twist and serve.

Ice

2 oz Punt e Mes or other Italian vermouth

2 oz Campari

2 oz gin, preferably Plymouth

1 orange twist

MAKES 1 DRINK

66 Be gentle when you muddle. With leaves, you're trying to bruise and release essential oils. With citrus, you want to both remove the flavorful oils from the peel and extract the juice. **99**

TABLA BARTENDER

mojito

Legends surrounding the origin of the mojito include pirates and plunder, but the first recipes for this Cuban mint-lime-rum combo—popular at Blue Smoke—date from the 1930s.

Fill a rocks glass with ice. Muddle 8 of the mint sprigs, the simple syrup, and the lime juice in a cocktail shaker until the mint is broken up. Add ice to the shaker and then the rum and shake vigorously. Strain into the glass, garnish with the remaining mint sprig and the lime wheel, and serve.

Ice

9 sprigs fresh mint

Splash of Simple Syrup (page 214)

1 oz fresh lime juice

2 oz golden rum, preferably Montecristo 12 Year

1 lime wheel

MAKES 1 DRINK

dark & stormy

Gosling's Black Seal rum and Barritt's spicy ginger beer are de rigueur in authentic versions of this no-nonsense cocktail, the national drink of Bermuda and a favorite among Blue Smoke guests.

Fill a Collins glass with ice. Add the rum, top with the ginger beer, stir gently, and serve.

Ice

1½ oz dark rum, preferably Gosling's Black Seal

About 5 oz good-quality ginger beer such as Barritt's

MAKES 1 DRINK

adonis

Ice

2 oz Manzanilla sherry

1 oz Italian sweet vermouth

2 dashes orange bitters

1 orange crescent

MAKES 1 DRINK

In the late nineteenth century, the bartending profession achieved distinction at the Waldorf-Astoria Hotel. This cocktail was created there to commemorate the success of the drink's namesake Broadway musical, which opened in 1884 and ran for a record 500 consecutive performances.

Fill a mixing glass with ice. Add the sherry, vermouth, and bitters and stir with a bar spoon until cold. Strain into a chilled martini glass, garnish with the orange crescent, and serve.

moscow mule

Ice

1½ oz vodka

1½ oz Ginger-Lime Syrup
(page 215)

Dash of Angostura bitters

3 oz soda water, or to taste

1 lime wheel

1 slice peeled fresh ginger

MAKES 1 DRINK

With its ginger and vodka kick, this drink—invented
in Los Angeles in 1941 and now an Eleven Madison Park
favorite—launched vodka's popularity in the States.

Fill a pewter cup or rocks glass with ice. Add the vodka, ginger-lime syrup,
bitters, and soda water and stir gently. Garnish with the lime wheel and
ginger slice and serve.

new classics

These cocktails are the bartenders' polished riffs on familiar classics, forward thinking while remaining rooted in tradition. The new twist might be the introduction of an unusual flavor or an inspired garnish. Mirroring the focus of the restaurants' kitchens, many of these cocktails also emphasize seasonal ingredients.

While it is bold to call these drinks new classics, most have appeared on the menus year after year, and each has become a signature cocktail for loyal guests.

contents

peruvian 75

Combine the cachaça, lemon juice, simple syrup, and Champagne in a chilled flute. Garnish with the lemon twist and serve.

1 oz cachaça or pisco

¾ oz fresh lemon juice

½ oz Simple Syrup (page 214)

4 oz Champagne, chilled

1 lemon twist

MAKES 1 DRINK

st. germain 75

Fill a highball glass three-fourths full with ice. Add the gin, elderflower liqueur, lemon juice, and simple syrup and stir gently. Top with the Champagne and serve.

Ice

2 oz gin, preferably Hendrick's

2 oz St-Germain elderflower liqueur

½ oz fresh lemon juice

½ oz Simple Syrup (page 214)

2 oz Champagne

MAKES 1 DRINK

mortoni

This refreshing drink is a twist on the classic Negroni. Made with vodka instead of gin, it was Danny's father's favorite cocktail. First offered in loving tribute to Morton Meyer, it is now a crowd-pleasing favorite at Gramercy Tavern.

Ice

1 oz vodka, preferably Ketel One

1 oz Campari

1 oz tonic water, preferably Q Tonic

1 lime wedge

1 orange wedge

2 lemon wedges

MAKES 1 DRINK

Fill a rocks glass and a cocktail shaker with ice. Add the vodka and Campari to the shaker and shake vigorously. Strain into the glass, top with the tonic water, and squeeze the juice from the lime and orange wedges and 1 of the lemon wedges into the drink. Garnish with the remaining lemon wedge and serve.

66 Danny's reputation as a hospitality pioneer and trendsetter is legendary, and redefining classics is a hallmark of his kitchen. We take that same approach with cocktails. We try to bring something new to the dialogue, be it a riff on a classic or a novel flavor combination. 99

BLUE SMOKE BARTENDER

east side negroni

Eleven Madison Park's vodka-based take on a classic Negroni emphasizes both floral and earthy notes with orange flower water and Grand Marnier, and is a great cocktail to kick off a meal.

Fill a cocktail shaker with ice. Add the vodka, Campari, vermouth, orange flower water, and Grand Marnier and shake vigorously. Strain into a chilled martini glass. Garnish with the orange twist and serve.

Ice

1½ oz vodka

¾ oz Campari

¾ oz sweet vermouth

3 or 4 drops orange flower water

¼ oz Grand Marnier or other orange liqueur

1 orange twist

MAKES 1 DRINK

blue smoke bloody mary

Ice

2 lemon wedges

1 lime wedge

1½ teaspoons hot-pepper sauce, preferably Texas Pete

½ teaspoon Worcestershire sauce

½ teaspoon prepared horseradish, or to taste

¼ teaspoon Blue Smoke Magic Dust or pinch of cayenne pepper (optional)

4 oz tomato juice

1½ oz vodka, preferably Ketel One

MAKES 1 DRINK

When Blue Smoke debuted its brunch menu in 2007, many suggested it was just a ploy to get this Bloody Mary on the menu. Long a top after-hours staff "shift drink," this winner combines a pair of house favorites (Texas Pete hot sauce and Magic Dust seasoning) in one mean cocktail.

Place a few ice cubes in a rocks glass. In a cocktail shaker, combine the lemon and lime wedges, hot sauce, Worcestershire sauce, horseradish, and Magic Dust, if desired, and muddle lightly. Add the tomato juice and vodka to the shaker and shake vigorously. Strain into the glass and serve.

heirloom bloody mary

To create this seasonal cocktail, the bartenders at Union Square Cafe pilfer the kitchen's heirloom tomatoes, sourced from the nearby farmers' market. At its best in late summer, this brunch mainstay is made truly special by passing the tomatoes through a potato ricer rather than juicing them.

To make the tomato juice, pass the heirloom tomatoes through a potato ricer into a glass measuring pitcher, pressing on the solids with a spoon to extract as much juice as possible. Discard the solids. You need about 4 oz juice (reserve the remainder for another use). Cover and refrigerate the juice for at least 30 minutes before serving.

Add the vodka, lime juice, horseradish, hot-pepper sauce, salt, and black pepper to the chilled juice and stir to mix well. Taste and adjust the seasoning. Fill a highball glass halfway with ice. Thread the grape tomatoes onto a wooden skewer. Pour the tomato mixture over the ice, garnish the glass with the skewer, and serve.

4 large, very ripe heirloom tomatoes

2 oz vodka, preferably Ketel One

1 oz fresh lime juice

½ teaspoon freshly grated horseradish, or to taste

1 teaspoon green hot-pepper sauce such as Tabasco, or to taste

Sea salt and coarsely ground black pepper to taste

Ice

Grape, cherry, or heirloom toy box tomatoes, halved, for garnish

MAKES 1 DRINK

blue smoke martini

Splash of Scotch, preferably Laphroaig

Ice

3 oz vodka, preferably Stolichnaya, chilled

3 olives stuffed with blue cheese (see note)

MAKES 1 DRINK

The "rinse" of Scotch lends this martini a smoky flavor, while the blue cheese–stuffed olives add a pleasing tang. You can purchase the olives, or you can stuff them at home: pipe softened blue cheese, preferably Maytag Blue, into pitted Spanish Queen olives, as they do at Blue Smoke.

Pour the Scotch into a chilled martini glass, tilt the glass to coat the inside, and pour out the excess. Fill a cocktail shaker with ice. Add the vodka and shake vigorously. Strain into the coated glass. Drop the olives into the glass and serve with an oyster fork across the top of the glass, or garnish with the olives threaded onto a cocktail pick.

66 We love to introduce our guests to this martini. Its smokiness pairs well with barbecue, and the olives stuffed with blue cheese are addictive. 99

BLUE SMOKE BARTENDER

the modern martini

Fresh lime and a cilantro infusion highlight the refreshing, herbaceous qualities of the original gin martini in this updated version served at The Modern.

Thread the lime wedge and the cherry tomato onto a small skewer. Fill a cocktail shaker with ice. Add the gin and lime juice and shake vigorously. Strain into a chilled martini glass, garnish with the skewer, and serve.

cilantro-infused gin Remove and discard the stems from the cilantro. In a large glass jar, combine the gin and cilantro leaves. Cover and let stand in a cool, dark place for 48 hours. Strain into a clean bottle, cap tightly, and store in a cool, dark place for up to 6 months.

1 lime wedge

1 cherry tomato

Ice

3½ oz Cilantro-Infused Gin (recipe follows)

½ oz fresh lime juice

MAKES 1 DRINK

CILANTRO-INFUSED GIN

1 large bunch (about 1 cup) fresh cilantro

1 bottle (750 ml) gin, preferably Tanqueray

MAKES 1 BOTTLE (750 ML)

pomegranate gimlet

Ice
1¾ oz gin, preferably Plymouth
1 oz fresh lime juice
1 oz fresh pomegranate juice
¾ oz Simple Syrup (page 214)
1 lime wheel
Pomegranate seeds for garnish

MAKES 1 DRINK

The pomegranate gimlet is a popular winter pour at Tabla. Each season brings a new fruit stand-in for the pomegranate: in fall, it's pear; in spring, strawberries; and in summer, peaches.

Fill a highball glass with ice. Add the gin, lime and pomegranate juices, and simple syrup and stir to blend. Garnish with the lime wheel, sprinkle a few pomegranate seeds on top, and serve.

" Pick any ingredients you like from your spice drawer—seeds, herbs, roots—and try infusing them in a high-proof vodka or a flavor-based spirit like whiskey. "

TABLA BARTENDER

ginger tonic

If there is one cocktail that has stood the test of time at Gramercy Tavern, this is it. Refreshing and delicious, it is a gin drink for the non-gin drinker.

Fill a tulip or pint glass with crushed ice. Add the gin and tonic water and stir gently. Garnish with the crystallized ginger and serve.

ginger-lime infused gin Put the ginger pieces in a large glass jar. Halve the limes and juice them, adding the juice and rinds to the jar with the ginger. Add the ginger-lime syrup and gin. Cover and refrigerate for at least 24 hours or up to 3 days. Strain into a clean bottle, cap tightly, and store in a cool, dark place for up to 1 month.

Crushed ice

3 oz Ginger-Lime Infused Gin
(recipe follows)

1 oz tonic water, preferably Q Tonic

Crystallized ginger for garnish

MAKES 1 DRINK

GINGER-LIME INFUSED GIN

6 oz fresh ginger, peeled and cut
into 2-inch pieces

3 limes

6 oz Ginger-Lime Syrup (page 215)

1 bottle (1 l) gin,
preferably Plymouth

MAKES ABOUT 36 OZ,
OR ENOUGH FOR 12 DRINKS

the madison parksider

This signature cocktail at Eleven Madison Park was created to be great with gin, but it's equally enjoyable as a nonalcoholic refresher.

Fill a Collins glass with ice. Muddle the cucumber segments in a cocktail shaker. Squeeze in the juice from the lime half. Add ice to the shaker and then the gin and simple syrup and shake vigorously. Strain into the glass, top with the soda water, and serve.

Ice

6 cucumber segments, cut into 1-inch cubes, about ½ cup

½ lime

1½ oz gin

¾ oz Simple Syrup (page 214)

4 oz soda water

MAKES 1 DRINK

margarita swizzle

Crushed ice

1½ oz silver tequila, preferably El Tesoro or other lowland tequila

½ oz fresh lime juice

½ oz fresh lemon juice

½ oz agave nectar

½ oz triple sec, preferably Luxardo Triplum, or other orange liqueur

¼ oz Velvet Falernum (clove-spiced liqueur)

Splash of fresh tangerine juice

3 drops Angostura bitters

1 lime wheel

MAKES 1 DRINK

In the Caribbean, bartenders often "swizzle" rum-based drinks by quickly rotating a long, forked tool—the original swizzle stick—between their palms in a crushed-ice cocktail to create a frosted glass and an icy-cold drink. Using the same technique with a bar spoon results in a perfectly chilled margarita.

Fill a highball glass with crushed ice. Add the tequila, lime and lemon juices, agave nectar, triple sec, Velvet Falernum, tangerine juice, and bitters. Stir briskly with a bar spoon until the glass is frosty. Thread the lime wheel onto a sipping straw, garnish the drink, and serve.

> **"** Proper shaking is vigorous and should sound almost like a machine gun, rapid and intense. A bad cocktail shake is like a bad handshake, limp and unimpressive. **"** — TABLA BARTENDER

cherry blossom sling

Ice

3 Brandied Cherries (page 219), plus a splash of their liquid

3 lime wedges, plus 1 for garnish (optional)

1½ oz gin

¾ oz Cherry Heering

½ oz Simple Syrup (page 214)

¼ oz fresh lime juice

Splash of soda water

Dash of Angostura bitters

Cherry blossoms for garnish (optional)

MAKES 1 DRINK

This popular sipper was created at Eleven Madison Park in homage to the legendary Singapore Sling. It uses the often-overlooked Cherry Heering, Denmark's venerable liqueur.

Fill a pilsner or highball glass with ice. Muddle the cherries and lime wedges in a cocktail shaker. Add ice to the shaker and then the gin, Cherry Heering, simple syrup, lime juice, and the splash of brandied cherry liquid and shake vigorously. Strain into the glass and top with the soda water and bitters. Garnish with the cherry blossoms and lime wedge, if desired, and serve.

piña limonada

What can you do with leftover ingredients from cooking? Take a cue from Union Square Cafe, whose bartenders nabbed the pastry chef's extra pineapple and invented a delicious new cocktail with a strikingly elegant garnish.

Fill a cocktail shaker with ice. Add the limonada and rum and shake vigorously. Strain into a chilled martini glass; there should be a creamy froth on top of the drink. Garnish with the pineapple chip and serve.

homemade limonada   In a large saucepan, combine the pineapple cubes, sugar, ginger, 1½ cups of the pineapple juice, and the water and bring to a boil over medium-high heat. Reduce the heat to maintain a moderate simmer and cook for 20 minutes. Remove from the heat and let cool to room temperature. Strain the liquid through a fine-mesh sieve into a large glass jar and discard the solids. Add the remaining ¼ cup pineapple juice and the lemon juice. The limonada will keep, tightly covered in the refrigerator, for up to 1 week.

NEW CLASSICS

Ice

3 oz Homemade Limonada (recipe follows)

2 oz white rum, preferably Bacardi Silver

1 dried pineapple chip

MAKES 1 DRINK

HOMEMADE LIMONADA

1 very ripe fresh pineapple, peeled, cored, and diced

1 cup raw sugar

2½ oz fresh ginger, peeled and grated

1¾ cups fresh pineapple juice, or good-quality, purchased pineapple juice

½ cup water

¼ cup fresh lemon juice

MAKES ABOUT 24 OZ, OR ENOUGH FOR 8 DRINKS

shot in the dark

1 lemon wedge and
raw sugar for rim

Ice

1½ oz light rum, preferably Cruzan
or Rhum Clément

½ oz fresh lemon juice

½ oz Simple Syrup (page 214)

4 oz good-quality ginger beer such
as Reed's Premium

About ¼ oz dark rum, preferably
Gosling's Black Seal

MAKES 1 DRINK

This visually stunning cocktail is a lighter take on the classic Dark & Stormy (page 38). To make a float, pour the finishing liquor slowly over the back of a spoon.

Moisten the outside edge of a highball glass with the lemon wedge. Sprinkle a little raw sugar on a small plate and dip the moistened rim in the sugar to coat it lightly. Fill the glass and a cocktail shaker with ice. Add the light rum, lemon juice, and simple syrup to the shaker and shake vigorously. Strain into the prepared glass and top with the ginger beer. Float the dark rum on top by pouring it over the back of a bar spoon into the glass and serve.

cranberry daiquiri

This vibrant drink—an inspired blend of sweet and spicy, with a wintry mix of cranberries, cinnamon, and orange zest—is Gramercy Tavern's best-selling cocktail, ever.

Crushed ice and ice cubes

1½ tablespoons Drunken Cranberries (page 219), plus 1 oz of their liquid

2 oz dark rum, preferably Gosling's

1 oz fresh lime juice

MAKES 1 DRINK

Place a small amount of crushed ice in a chilled martini glass. Add 1 tablespoon of the drunken cranberries. Fill a cocktail shaker with ice cubes. Add the rum, the 1 oz drunken cranberry liquid, and the lime juice to the shaker and shake vigorously. Strain into the prepared glass. Thread the remaining drunken cranberries onto a small skewer or float on top and serve.

> **"** You can make any drink taste better with bitters. Using them is like using specialized salts in cooking. They let you remain true to the original cocktail while giving it a completely new spin. **"**
>
> TABLA BARTENDER

east india daiquiri

A classic daiquiri combines rum with lime and simple syrup. Eleven Madison Park took that popular summer standard into fall with clove-spiced Velvet Falernum liqueur and fragrant Earl Grey tea.

Fill a cocktail shaker with ice. Add the rum, tea, Velvet Falernum, lime juice, and bitters and shake vigorously. Strain into a chilled martini glass and garnish with cherries. Top with a dusting of grated nutmeg and serve.

Ice

1½ oz golden rum

1½ oz brewed Earl Grey tea, chilled

1 oz Velvet Falernum (clove-spiced liqueur)

¾ oz fresh lime juice

Dash of Underberg bitters

Fresh cherries and freshly grated nutmeg for garnish

MAKES 1 DRINK

rum & rye old-fashioned

Most rum is distilled from fermented molasses (a by-product of sugar-making), but high-quality *rhum agricole*, which is manufactured in the French West Indies, is made from fresh-squeezed sugarcane juice.

Ice

1 oz golden rum, preferably *rhum agricole*

1 oz rye whiskey

¼ oz Demerara Simple Syrup (recipe follows)

2 drops Angostura bitters

1 orange twist

MAKES 1 DRINK

DEMERARA SIMPLE SYRUP

1 cup demerara sugar

½ cup water

MAKES ABOUT 1 CUP

Fill a mixing glass and a rocks glass with ice. Add the rum, rye, demerara syrup, and bitters to the mixing glass and stir with a bar spoon until cold. Strain into the rocks glass, garnish with the orange twist, and serve.

demerara simple syrup In a saucepan, combine the sugar and water and bring to a boil over medium-high heat, stirring until the sugar is dissolved. Remove from the heat and let cool. Pour into a clean bottle. The syrup will keep, tightly capped in the refrigerator, for up to 2 weeks.

66 Our smoky bacon-and-nut mix (page 191) is perfect with a wintry bourbon-based drink. The combination of orange and salt is outstanding and almost as addictive as the nuts themselves! 99

HUDSON YARDS CHEF

the modern old-fashioned

Choose ripe yet slightly firm Bosc pears to add the perfect mellow note to this seasonal spin on the standard. Use a mandoline to make an ultrathin slice for an elegant garnish.

In a small bowl, soak 3 of the dried cherries in ½ oz of the Poire William until plump. Thread the cherries onto a small skewer and set aside. Fill a rocks glass with ice. Muddle 4 of the pear slices, the remaining dried cherry, and the lemon juice in a cocktail shaker. Add ice and then the bourbon, the remaining 1 oz Poire William, the simple syrup, and the bitters and shake vigorously. Strain into the glass, garnish with the skewered cherries and the remaining pear slice, and serve.

4 dried cherries

1½ oz Poire William
or other pear liqueur

Ice

5 slices ripe but firm red Bosc pear

Splash of fresh lemon juice

2 oz bourbon, preferably Michter's

½ oz Simple Syrup (page 214)

Dash of Angostura bitters

MAKES 1 DRINK

inspired flavors

Some of the most innovative cocktails dreamed up by the bartenders at Danny Meyer's restaurants are inspired by the flavors from the kitchens.

Combining flavors in cocktails, just as in cooking, is an art. Start with fresh, high-quality ingredients—seasonal produce, just-squeezed juices, freshly grated spices—and you'll be well on your way. Whether it's a unique marriage of flavors, such as rhubarb and peppercorns, or of spirits, like sherry and absinthe, the union will guarantee a memorable sip.

contents

forza totti

Inspired by the classic Lemon Drop and named after Italian soccer star Francesco Totti, this popular Union Square Cafe cocktail uses homemade limoncello and grappa to add a nutty backbone and kick of flavor.

If using the Lemon Dust, moisten the outside edge of a chilled martini glass with the lemon wedge. Sprinkle a little Lemon Dust on a small plate and dip the moistened rim in the sugar to coat it lightly. Place 1½ oz crushed ice in the bottom of a martini glass and fill a cocktail shaker with ice cubes. Add the limoncello to the shaker and shake vigorously. Strain into the martini glass, top with the grappa, and serve.

homemade limoncello Using a sharp knife or a vegetable peeler, remove the yellow zest from all the lemons, making sure to leave the bitter white pith behind. Place the zest in a 1-gallon glass jar with a lid. Peel off all the remaining white pith from 2½ of the lemons (reserve the remaining lemons for another use). Discard the pith and coarsely chop the pulp. Add the pulp and the vodka to the jar. Cover and let stand in a cool, dark place for 1 week, shaking the jar once or twice a day. After 1 week, add the simple syrup and lemon juice, stirring well. Cover and let stand in a cool, dark place for 4 more days. Strain into a clean bottle, cap tightly, and store in a cool, dark place for up to 6 months.

INSPIRED FLAVORS

1 lemon wedge and Lemon Dust (page 217) for rim (optional)

Crushed ice and ice cubes

3 oz Homemade Limoncello (recipe follows)

¾ oz best-quality grappa such as Grappa di Brunello di Montalcino

MAKES 1 DRINK

HOMEMADE LIMONCELLO

12 lemons

1 bottle (750 ml) vodka, preferably Ketel One

2 cups Simple Syrup (page 214)

1 cup fresh lemon juice

MAKES ABOUT 48 OZ,
OR ENOUGH FOR 16 DRINKS

payback

2 slices jalapeño chile

Ice

½ fresh kiwifruit, peeled and sliced

1½ oz silver tequila, preferably Gran Centenario

1 oz triple sec, preferably Luxardo Triplum

½ oz fresh lemon juice

½ oz fresh lime juice

½ oz Simple Syrup (page 214)

MAKES 1 DRINK

Seek out a smooth tequila like Gran Centenario for this balanced cocktail, with its lively notes of hot, sweet, and tart. Fresh kiwifruit pairs deliciously with chile and lends visual interest to this favorite drink at The Modern.

Using a small knife, remove and discard the seeds from the jalapeño slices, but leave the white membrane. Fill a rocks glass with ice. Muddle the jalapeño and kiwifruit slices in a cocktail shaker. Add ice to the shaker and then the tequila, triple sec, lemon and lime juices, and simple syrup and shake vigorously. Strain into the glass and serve.

thai basil bliss

In this luscious cocktail, the pineapple is a backdrop to the sweet, spicy Thai basil, which pervades the glass with a wonderful herbal presence.

4 fresh Thai basil leaves, plus 1 leaf for garnish

Four 1-inch cubes fresh pineapple

Ice

½ oz Simple Syrup (page 214)

2 oz silver tequila, preferably Patrón

¾ oz fresh lime juice

Splash of Champagne (optional)

MAKES 1 DRINK

Muddle 4 of the basil leaves and the pineapple in a cocktail shaker. Add ice to the shaker and then the simple syrup, tequila, and lime juice and shake vigorously. Strain into a chilled martini glass and add the splash of Champagne, if desired. Garnish with the remaining basil leaf and serve.

66 This cocktail brings fresh fruit and Tabla's flair to a margarita. Use a fistful of Thai basil leaves and make sure they are perfectly fresh. Muddle the basil with chunks of pineapple into a complete paste before you add the rest of the ingredients. 99

TABLA BARTENDER

golden skirt swizzle

To make the cucumber juice for this refreshing take on the lemon-lime margarita, use an electric juicer, or process peeled cucumber in a blender and then press the pulp through a fine-mesh sieve, capturing the juice in a bowl.

Fill a highball glass with crushed ice. Add the tequila, lime and lemon juices, agave nectar, triple sec, Velvet Falernum, cucumber and tangerine juices, and bitters. Stir briskly with a bar spoon until the glass is frosty. Garnish with the kiwifruit slices and serve.

Crushed ice

1½ oz silver tequila, preferably
El Tesoro or other lowland tequila

½ oz fresh lime juice

½ oz fresh lemon juice

½ oz agave nectar

½ oz triple sec, preferably Luxardo
Triplum, or other orange liqueur

¼ oz Velvet Falernum
(clove-spiced liqueur)

1 teaspoon fresh cucumber juice

Splash of fresh tangerine juice

3 drops of Angostura bitters

2–4 slices peeled fresh golden
or regular kiwifruit

MAKES 1 DRINK

rickshaw

A Gramercy classic, the Rickshaw is an ideal party drink. It was created to make gin fun by using flavor components that showcase the spirit's light and refreshing character.

Crushed ice and ice cubes
2 oz gin
1 oz fresh lime juice
1 oz Basil Syrup (page 215)
Fresh basil leaves for garnish

MAKES 1 DRINK

Fill a rocks glass with crushed ice and a cocktail shaker with ice cubes. Add the gin, lime juice, and basil syrup to the shaker and shake vigorously. Strain into the glass, garnish with basil leaves, and serve.

kachumber kooler

Inspired by a chopped salad commonly found at roadside food stands in Chef Floyd Cardoz's native India, this Tabla classic is aromatic and invigorating.

Fill a highball glass with ice. Muddle 2 slices of the cucumber, the chile piece, and the cilantro in a cocktail shaker. Add ice to the shaker and then the gin, lime juice, and simple syrup and shake vigorously. Strain into the glass, garnish with the remaining cucumber slice, and serve.

Ice

3 slices English cucumber

One 1½-inch piece green Calistan chile or other slender green chile

1 sprig fresh cilantro

1¾ oz gin, preferably Plymouth

½ oz fresh lime juice

½ oz Simple Syrup (page 214)

MAKES 1 DRINK

INSPIRED FLAVORS

glass slipper

In this cocktail inspired by the Vesper martini James Bond orders in *Casino Royale,* the vanilla infusion heightens the botanical profile of the gin and complements the honeyed character of both the Lillet and the yellow Chartreuse.

Fill a cocktail shaker with ice and add the gin, Chartreuse, and Lillet. Stir well and strain into a chilled martini glass. Garnish with the orange twist and serve.

vanilla-infused gin   In a large glass jar, combine the vanilla beans and gin. Cover and let stand in a cool, dark place for 2–4 days. Strain into a clean bottle, cap tightly, and store in a cool, dark place for up to 6 months.

Ice

2 oz Vanilla-Infused Gin (recipe follows)

¼ oz yellow Chartreuse

¼ oz Lillet Blanc

1 orange twist

MAKES 1 DRINK

VANILLA-INFUSED GIN

2 vanilla beans, preferably Tahitian, split lengthwise

1 bottle (1 l) gin, preferably Tanqueray

MAKES 1 BOTTLE (1 L)

Crushed ice

1 oz Spiced Rhubarb Syrup (recipe follows)

5 oz Prosecco, chilled

Rhubarb strip for garnish

MAKES 1 DRINK

SPICED RHUBARB SYRUP

4 cups diced rhubarb, cut into
¼-inch cubes (about 10 stalks total)

4 cups Simple Syrup (page 214)

1-inch piece fresh ginger,
peeled and diced

2 tablespoons whole black peppercorns

Zest of 1 lime, cut into strips

1 vanilla bean, split lengthwise

¾ oz spiced rum, preferably
Captain Morgan Original

MAKES 10 OZ,
OR ENOUGH FOR 10 DRINKS

rhubarb sparkler

In this sparkling Gramercy springtime cocktail, the use of tart rhubarb to complement the spiced rum and sweet vanilla echoes the seasonal flavors used in the kitchen.

Fill a flute with crushed ice. Add the spiced rhubarb syrup and the Prosecco. Garnish with the rhubarb strip and serve.

spiced rhubarb syrup Place the rhubarb in a nonreactive bowl or container with a tight-fitting lid. In a saucepan, combine the simple syrup, ginger, peppercorns, lime zest, and vanilla bean. Warm over medium-high heat until the mixture is nearly boiling, 8–10 minutes. Remove from the heat and let cool. Strain the syrup mixture over the rhubarb. Add a few pieces of the ginger and the vanilla bean to the bowl and discard the remaining solids. Cover and let stand for 10 minutes, swirling the bowl occasionally to evenly coat the fruit. Add the rum, cover, and refrigerate for at least 4 hours or up to 1 week.

hibiscus mojito

Dried hibiscus blossoms impart a fragrant, sweet-tart flavor and a lovely deep pink color to drinks. Look for them under the name *jamaica* flowers in Latin markets.

Fill a cocktail shaker and a double rocks glass with ice. Add the rum, hibiscus syrup, and lime and lemon juices to the shaker and shake vigorously. Strain into the glass, garnish with the lime wheel, and serve.

hibiscus simple syrup In a saucepan, combine the sugar and water and bring to a boil over medium heat, stirring until the sugar is dissolved. Remove from the heat and stir in the dried hibiscus flowers. Let stand at room temperature for 10 minutes. Strain into a glass jar, cover, and refrigerate until needed. The syrup will keep, tightly covered in the refrigerator, for up to 2 weeks.

Ice

2 oz white rum

2 oz Hibiscus Simple Syrup (recipe follows)

½ oz fresh lime juice

½ oz fresh lemon juice

1 lime wheel

MAKES 1 DRINK

HIBISCUS SIMPLE SYRUP

⅔ cup sugar

⅔ cup water

¼ cup dried hibiscus flowers

MAKES ¾ CUP

cp daiquiri

¼ oz Pernod or other anise liqueur

6 fresh curry leaves, plus 1 for garnish

Ice

2 oz white rum

1 oz fresh lime juice

1 oz Simple Syrup (page 214)

MAKES 1 DRINK

Fresh curry leaves, an ingredient used often in Tabla's kitchen, carry a heady aroma. Paired with Pernod (hence, the CP), they put a spicy, citrusy spin on this lime favorite. Curry leaves look similar to tiny bay leaves and can be found in Indian markets and specialty-food stores.

Pour the Pernod into a chilled martini glass, tilt the glass to coat the inside, and pour out any excess. Muddle 6 of the curry leaves in a cocktail shaker. Add ice and the rum, lime juice, and simple syrup and shake vigorously. Strain into the coated glass, garnish with the remaining curry leaf, and serve.

INSPIRED FLAVORS

tablatini

A perennial favorite at Tabla, this tropical potion delivers a touch of drama with its garnish of pineapple speared on a lemongrass stalk.

Fill a cocktail shaker with ice. Add the vodka, pineapple and lemon juices, and simple syrup and shake vigorously. Strain into a chilled martini glass. Squeeze the juice from the lemon wedge over the top, garnish with the lemongrass-skewered pineapple, and serve.

lemongrass-infused pineapple juice In a large saucepan, combine the pineapple, lemongrass, sugar, and water. Bring to a boil over medium heat, stirring until the sugar is dissolved. Reduce the heat to maintain a brisk simmer and cook for 5 minutes, stirring constantly. Remove from the heat and let cool slightly. Strain into a glass jar, pressing on the solids with the back of a spoon to extract the juices, and let cool. The juice will keep, tightly covered in the refrigerator, for up to 1 week.

Ice

1¾ oz citrus-infused vodka, preferably Absolut Citron

2 oz Lemongrass-Infused Pineapple Juice (recipe follows)

½ oz lemon juice

¼ oz Simple Syrup (page 214)

1 lemon wedge

1 small piece fresh pineapple skewered on a fresh lemongrass stalk

MAKES 1 DRINK

LEMONGRASS-INFUSED PINEAPPLE JUICE

1 fresh pineapple, peeled, cored, and finely diced

8 lemongrass stalks, roughly chopped, with tough tops and bottoms trimmed

¾ cup sugar

1½ cups water

MAKES ABOUT 3 CUPS, OR ENOUGH FOR 12 DRINKS

66 This signature cocktail
was invented to go with a
variety of flavors and spices
found on Tabla's menu. Its
balance of sweetness and
acidity mirrors the dynamic
found in many of Chef
Cardoz's dishes. 99

TABLA BARTENDER

lots o'passion

A longtime Tabla classic, this enjoyably tangy drink charms nearly everyone with its exotic flavor palate.

Ice
1¾ oz vodka
¾ oz Cointreau or other orange liqueur
1 oz cranberry juice
½ oz fresh lime juice
½ oz Passion Fruit Purée, homemade (page 218) or purchased
½ oz Simple Syrup (page 214)
1 lime wheel

MAKES 1 DRINK

Fill a cocktail shaker with ice. Add the vodka, Cointreau, cranberry and lime juices, passion fruit purée, and simple syrup and shake vigorously. Strain into a chilled martini glass, garnish with the lime wheel, and serve.

yuzu friendly

The pleasantly sour, citrusy flavor of yuzu brightens this cocktail, which complements the Indian spices showcased on Tabla's menu. Shop for the marmalade at Asian markets.

Ice
2 oz vodka
1 oz Lillet Blanc
1 oz yuzu-honey marmalade
1 orange twist

MAKES 1 DRINK

Fill a cocktail shaker with ice. Add the vodka, Lillet, and marmalade and shake vigorously, making sure the marmalade dissolves completely. Strain into a chilled martini glass, garnish with the orange twist, and serve.

cucumber caipiroska

The Modern pays homage to the classic Brazilian Caipirinha in this aromatic and alluring drink that pairs citrus with cucumber.

Fill a rocks glass with ice. Muddle the cucumber slices and lemon wedge in a cocktail shaker. Add ice to the shaker and then the vodka, lemon juice, and simple syrup and shake vigorously. Strain into the glass, garnish with cucumber slices, and serve.

Ice

2 slices English cucumber, plus extra for garnish

1 lemon wedge

1½ oz citrus-flavored vodka, preferably Hangar One Buddha's Hand Citron

½ oz fresh lemon juice

½ oz Simple Syrup (page 214)

MAKES 1 DRINK

the modern toddy

Fuyu persimmon contributes a bright garnish to this warming drink that combines applejack with lemon verbena for a thoroughly modern take on a hot toddy.

¼ teaspoon clover honey

10 dried lemon verbena leaves

3 oz boiling water

1½ oz applejack, preferably Laird's, or other apple brandy

1 oz apple schnapps, preferably Berentzen Apfelkorn

¼ oz Velvet Falernum (clove-spiced liqueur)

Splash of fresh lemon juice

1 slice Fuyu persimmon

MAKES 1 DRINK

Place the honey in the bottom of a teapot with an infuser. Crush the dried lemon verbena leaves and add to the infuser. Pour in the boiling water and let steep for 5 minutes. Remove the infuser and add the applejack, schnapps, and Velvet Falernum. Stir to mix, then pour into a glass mug. Add the lemon juice, garnish with the persimmon slice, and serve.

red delicious

A trio of apple-derived liquids—freshly pressed apple cider, low-alcohol apple liqueur, and high-octane distilled apple brandy—combine to create this seductive drink that is the ultimate expression of apples.

Moisten the outside edge of a chilled martini glass with the lemon wedge. Sprinkle a little cinnamon sugar on a small plate and dip the moistened rim in the sugar to coat it lightly. Fill a cocktail shaker with ice. Add the applejack, apple cider, pommeau, crème de cassis, and lemon juice to the shaker and shake vigorously. Strain into the prepared glass, garnish with the star anise, and serve.

1 lemon wedge and Cinnamon Sugar (page 217) for rim

Ice

1½ oz applejack, preferably Laird's, or other apple brandy

1½ oz natural or unsweetened apple cider

½ oz pommeau (French apple aperitif)

½ oz crème de cassis

¼ oz fresh lemon juice

1 star anise pod

MAKES 1 DRINK

smashing lady

Tiny Lady apples are available at farmers' markets and specialty-produce markets in fall, when this cocktail can be found on The Modern's menu.

In a cocktail shaker, muddle the apple slices and simple syrup. Add several ice cubes and the applejack and lemon juice and shake vigorously. Pour into a highball glass. Top with soda water and serve with a spoon straw ("stroon").

1 Lady apple, quartered, cored, and cut into five ½-inch slices

¾ oz Simple Syrup (page 214)

Ice

1½ oz applejack, preferably Laird's, or other apple brandy

¾ oz fresh lemon juice

Soda water to taste

MAKES 1 DRINK

grey gardens

During the nearby Broadway run of its namesake musical, this cocktail was served at The Modern's sister cafe, Terrace 5, located within MoMA's galleries. Only the Spanish sherry producer Lustau offers a *solera*-aged wine made from the uncommon red Tintilla de Rota grape, a true rarity worth seeking out.

Fill a highball glass and a cocktail shaker with ice. Add the Scotch, sherry, bitters, and simple syrup to the shaker and shake vigorously. Strain into the glass, top with the tea, and stir to blend. Garnish with the lemon wedge and serve.

Ice

1½ oz blended Scotch whisky, preferably Famous Grouse or other smooth, sweet Scotch

½ oz sherry, preferably Emilio Lustau Tintilla de Rota or a fruit-forward sherry made from Moscatel grapes

2 dashes of Angostura bitters

¼ oz Simple Syrup (page 214)

4 oz brewed Earl Grey tea, chilled

1 lemon wedge

MAKES 1 DRINK

Ice

1½ oz blended Scotch whisky,
such as J&B

1½ oz brewed English
Breakfast tea, chilled

¾ oz sweetened condensed milk

Smoked tea leaves for garnish

MAKES 1 DRINK

the guilty kilt

In this smoke-laden Scottish libation, Eleven Madison
Park took an innovative approach to serving tea. Here
it's married with peaty Scotch and a sprinkle of tea
leaves for a creamy, sweet infusion.

Fill a rocks glass and a cocktail shaker with ice. Add the Scotch, tea, and
condensed milk to the shaker and shake vigorously. Strain into the glass
and garnish with smoked tea leaves.

INSPIRED FLAVORS

winter vacation

Ice

1½ oz blended Scotch whisky

¾ oz crème de violette

¾ oz fresh lemon juice

¾ oz Lavender Syrup (page 214)

1 lavender sprig or lavender
ice cube (optional)

MAKES 1 DRINK

This cocktail combines Scotch with two floral elements
for a departure from the usual heavy winter drinks. For a
special touch, make lavender ice cubes: place the fresh
blossoms in ice cube trays, fill with water, and freeze.

Fill a rocks glass and a cocktail shaker with ice. Add the Scotch, crème de violette,
lemon juice, and lavender syrup to the shaker and shake vigorously. Strain into
the glass, garnish with the lavender sprig and ice cube, if desired, and serve.

rye smile

Ice

2 oz Ginger-Infused Rye
(recipe follows)

1 oz fresh lemon juice

1 oz Simple Syrup (page 214)

Soda water to taste

1 piece crystallized ginger

MAKES 1 DRINK

GINGER-INFUSED RYE

8 oz fresh ginger, peeled and sliced

1 bottle (750 ml) rye whiskey,
preferably Old Overholt

MAKES 1 BOTTLE (750 ML)

Robust rye whiskey all but disappeared during Prohibition.
Thankfully, it has been revived by specialty producers and
is profiled in this ginger-infused Tabla creation.

Fill a double rocks glass and a cocktail shaker with ice. Add the rye, lemon juice,
and simple syrup to the shaker and shake vigorously. Strain into the glass and top
with soda water. Garnish with the crystallized ginger and serve.

ginger-infused rye Lightly smash the ginger slices with the flat side of a
knife blade. In a large glass jar or pitcher, combine the ginger and rye. Let stand
at room temperature for at least 24 hours. Strain into a clean bottle, discarding
the ginger. Cap tightly and store in a cool, dark place for up to 6 months.

elegant sips

Some cocktails are effortlessly elegant. It might be the stylish way the drink is prepared or presented. Or, it might come from the use of a singular spirit, such as sherry, an ingredient that typifies panache, like rose petals, or simply the graceful introduction of Champagne.

These elegant cocktails conjure up images of intimate gatherings or important occasions. Smooth, sophisticated, and sexy, these drinks are showstoppers that will spark a celebration.

contents

coming up roses

This popular cocktail at The Modern reinterprets the mojito.
It uses rum as the base spirit and lime as the citrus component,
but substitutes fresh rose petals for the mint leaves and
Champagne for the soda.

3 lime wedges

4 fresh rose petals

½ oz rose syrup, preferably Monin

Dash of rose water, preferably
Al Wadi

Ice

2 oz raspberry-flavored rum,
preferably Bacardi Razz

2 oz Champagne

MAKES 1 DRINK

Muddle the lime wedges, rose petals, rose syrup, and rose water in a cocktail shaker.
Add ice to the shaker and then the rum and shake vigorously. Pour into a highball glass,
top with the Champagne, and serve.

> **"** Red roses have long symbolized beauty, and this gorgeous cocktail evokes that allure. It's quite striking, refreshing, and flavorful. **"**
>
> THE MODERN BARTENDER

a fino introduction

This aperitif-like cocktail highlights the delicate aromas of Fino, the driest and lightest style of sherry. Manzanilla, made near the coastal town of Sanlúcar de Barrameda, is a type of Fino that's especially light yet quite flavorful, making it an excellent choice here.

Combine the sherry, vermouths, and maraschino liqueur in a mixing glass. Add the 2 drops bitters, or to taste. Add ice and stir with a bar spoon until cold. Strain into a sherry glass, garnish with the lemon twist, and serve.

2½ oz Fino sherry, preferably Manzanilla

½ oz dry vermouth

½ oz sweet vermouth, preferably Carpano Antica

¼ oz maraschino liqueur, preferably Luxardo

2 drops Angostura bitters, or to taste

Ice

1 lemon twist

MAKES 1 DRINK

ramos verjus fizz

Ice

2 oz whole milk

1¼ oz Simple Syrup (page 214)

1 oz *verjus*, preferably Wölffer

1½ oz gin, preferably Junípero

2 drops orange flower water

1 teaspoon egg white

Soda water to taste

MAKES 1 DRINK

Verjus—"green juice"—is unfermented juice pressed from unripe grapes that adds a delicate tartness to this traditional fizz. Look for it from producers such as New York's Wölffer Estate Vineyards.

Fill a cocktail shaker with ice. Add the milk, simple syrup, *verjus*, gin, orange flower water, and egg white and shake vigorously. Strain into a highball glass, top with soda water, and serve.

turf race

Ice
3½ oz gin, preferably Hendrick's
½ oz maraschino liqueur,
preferably Luxardo
½ oz absinthe, preferably Lucid
1 generous dash of orange bitters,
preferably Fee Brothers
1 orange twist

MAKES 1 DRINK

This complex, aromatic cocktail from Gramercy Tavern, a savvy adaptation of one historically served at London's Savoy Hotel, celebrates absinthe's return to the United States. Make sure to "twist" the orange twist into the glass to capture all its essential oils.

Fill a cocktail shaker with ice. Add the gin, maraschino liqueur, absinthe, and bitters and shake vigorously. Strain into a chilled martini glass, garnish with the orange twist, and serve.

125

ELEGANT SIPS

the remedy

Ice
1½ oz gin
¾ oz fresh lemon juice
¾ oz Ginger-Honey Syrup
(page 214)
1 slice crystallized ginger

MAKES 1 DRINK

Keep the delicious ginger-honey syrup used in this cocktail on hand to cure whatever ails you. It is as restorative stirred into tea as it is shaken into this piquant drink.

Fill a cocktail shaker with ice. Add the gin, lemon juice, and ginger-honey syrup and shake vigorously. Strain into a chilled martini glass or an ice-filled rocks glass. Garnish with the crystallized ginger and serve.

23 skidoo

This popular Eleven Madison Park drink is named for the neighborhood police call number from the flapper era: on 23rd Street near the Flatiron Building, gusts of wind made women's short dresses billow, provoking plenty of gawking.

Ice

1 oz gin

½ oz St-Germain elderflower liqueur

¼ oz Lemon Thyme Syrup (page 215)

¼ oz fresh lemon juice

3 oz Champagne, chilled

1 sprig fresh lemon thyme (optional)

MAKES 1 DRINK

Fill a mixing glass with ice. Add the gin, elderflower liqueur, lemon thyme syrup, and lemon juice and stir with a bar spoon until cold. Strain into a flute and top with the Champagne. Garnish with the thyme sprig, if desired, and serve.

66 The name 23 Skidoo has come to symbolize our proprietary, seasonal, sparkling cocktail. We offer variations of this drink throughout the year, all bearing the same name. 99

ELEVEN MADISON PARK BARTENDER

hang thyme

Beautifully aromatic and redolent of fresh thyme, this cocktail is both visually appealing—the floating bits of thyme are striking—and purely delicious in its simplicity.

Fill a rocks glass with ice. Muddle 4 of the thyme sprigs in a cocktail shaker. Add ice to the shaker and then the vodka, lime juice, and sugar and shake vigorously. Strain into the glass, garnish with the remaining thyme sprig, and serve.

Ice

5 sprigs fresh thyme

2 oz citrus-flavored vodka, preferably Hangar One Buddha's Hand Citron

1 oz fresh lime juice

1 oz sugar

MAKES 1 DRINK

66 Make sure the shaker is large enough to hold all of the ingredients and plenty of ice and still have room for everything to move around. 99

TABLA BARTENDER

heart of darkness

Ice

1½ oz chocolate-flavored vodka, preferably Van Gogh Dutch chocolate vodka

1 oz chocolate liqueur, preferably Godiva dark chocolate liqueur

½ oz Passion Fruit Purée, homemade (page 218) or purchased

Passion Fruit Gelée Cubes (page 219) for garnish

MAKES 1 DRINK

Some have said this luscious "liquid dessert," first served at Terrace 5, should really be called "Sweet and Vicious." The bold taste of passion fruit drives a contrasting note through two layers of chocolate and is decidedly sinful. For added drama, serve in a sugar-rimmed glass.

Fill a cocktail shaker with ice. Add the vodka, chocolate liqueur, and passion fruit purée and shake vigorously. Strain into a chilled martini glass. Thread cubes of passion fruit gelée onto a skewer, garnish the drink with the skewer, and serve.

131

ELEGANT SIPS

citrus gingersnap

With its wintry flavors of orange and ginger and its festive seasonal garnish of pomegranate seeds, this lightly sparkling cocktail is the ideal way to toast the holidays.

Fill a cocktail shaker with ice. Add the vodka, crème de gingembre, and simple syrup and shake vigorously. Strain into a chilled martini glass and top with the Champagne. Garnish with the orange wheel and pomegranate seeds, if desired, and serve.

Ice

1¼ oz orange-flavored vodka, preferably Stoli Orange

1¼ oz crème de gingembre, preferably Massenez, or other ginger liqueur

Splash of Simple Syrup (page 214)

Splash of Champagne

1 orange wheel

Pomegranate seeds for garnish (optional)

MAKES 1 DRINK

pointillist pêche

½ oz crème de pêche,
preferably Massenez

3–5 oz Prosecco Brut, chilled

MAKES 1 DRINK

Perfect for brunch, this sweet, sparkling drink was created at Terrace 5 to celebrate a MoMA exhibit of the work of pointillist painter Georges Seurat.

Pour the crème de pêche into a chilled flute. Top with the Prosecco and serve.

pc fizz

This refreshing drink is a take on a classic fizz, but trades out gin for Pimm's No. 1 and Chartreuse (hence, the PC). The double 30-second shake results in a frothier crown. For a variation, strain the mixture into a highball glass with no ice and top with 1½–2 ounces soda water.

Fill a highball glass with ice. Combine the Pimm's No. 1, Chartreuse, simple syrup, lemon and lime juices, and egg white in a cocktail shaker. Shake vigorously for 30 seconds. Add ice to the shaker and shake vigorously for another 30 seconds. Strain into the glass and serve.

Ice

1½ oz Pimm's No. 1

½ oz yellow Chartreuse

1 oz Simple Syrup (page 214)

¾ oz fresh lemon juice

¾ oz fresh lime juice

1 large egg white

MAKES 1 DRINK

winter solstice

Fill a cocktail shaker with ice. Add the brandy, pear nectar, and Grand Marnier and shake vigorously. Strain into a chilled martini glass, garnish with the rosemary sprig, and serve.

rosemary-infused pear nectar

In a jar, combine the pear nectar and rosemary. Cover and refrigerate for at least 12 hours or up to 2 days. Remove and discard the rosemary before using. The infused nectar will keep, covered in the refrigerator, for up to 4 days.

Ice

1¼ oz brandy

1¾ oz Rosemary-Infused Pear Nectar (recipe follows)

⅔ oz Grand Marnier or other orange liqueur

1 small sprig fresh rosemary

MAKES 1 DRINK

ROSEMARY-INFUSED PEAR NECTAR

1½ cups good-quality pear nectar such as Kern's

5 sprigs fresh rosemary

MAKES 1½ CUPS,
OR ENOUGH FOR 6 DRINKS

williams pear sour

Place 1 tablespoon of crushed ice in a chilled martini glass and top with the dried pear. Fill a cocktail shaker with ice cubes. Add the pear brandy, pear liqueur, and lemon juice to the shaker and shake vigorously. Strain into the prepared glass and serve.

Crushed ice and ice cubes

1 slice dried pear

1½ oz pear brandy, preferably Clear Creek

1 oz pear liqueur, preferably Belle de Brillet

1 oz fresh lemon juice

MAKES 1 DRINK

r&r

The name of this thirst-quenching summer cocktail from Gramercy Tavern plays on both "rest and relaxation" and "roses and raspberries." Try it over crushed ice as a julep alternative. The Tavern's bartenders add rose water with a medicine dropper to help fine-tune the drink's flavor.

Ice

8 raspberries

5 drops rose water

5½ oz Bourbon Sweet Tea
(recipe follows)

MAKES 1 DRINK

BOURBON SWEET TEA

3 cups brewed black tea, chilled

2 cups bourbon,
preferably Maker's Mark

½ cup Simple Syrup (page 214)

MAKES 5½ CUPS,
OR ENOUGH FOR 8 DRINKS

Fill a highball glass with ice. Thread 3 of the raspberries onto a small skewer and set aside. Put the remaining 5 raspberries in a cocktail shaker, add the 5 drops rose water, and muddle with the raspberries. Add ice and the bourbon sweet tea. Shake vigorously and strain into the glass. Garnish with the skewer and serve.

bourbon sweet tea   In a pitcher, combine the tea, bourbon, and simple syrup and stir to mix well. The tea will keep, covered in the refrigerator, for up to 3 days.

dream a little dream

Honey, lemon, and a base spirit are a traditional and comforting combination. Here, cardamom delivers a spot-on nuance to the subtle oakiness of rye whiskey.

Fill a cocktail shaker with ice. Add the rye, cardamom syrup, and lemon juice and shake vigorously. Strain into a chilled martini glass, garnish with the lemon twist and cardamom pod threaded on a metal skewer, and serve.

Ice

1½ oz rye whiskey

¾ oz Cardamom Syrup (page 215)

¾ oz fresh lemon juice

1 lemon twist

1 cardamom pod

MAKES 1 DRINK

> **66** We want our cocktail program to mirror what the chef is doing. It's rooted in the classics but forward thinking at the same time. **99**
>
> ELEVEN MADISON PARK BARTENDER

bee lavender

Ice
1¾ oz Scotch
1 oz lavender honey
¾ oz Lillet Blanc
¾ oz fresh lemon juice
1 sprig fresh lavender

MAKES 1 DRINK

The inspiration for this riff on the classic Bee's Knees came in part from the heady aromas of Chef Daniel Humm's legendary lavender-and-honey-glazed duck that waft through the kitchen in early spring, when this dish is a mainstay on the menu at Eleven Madison Park.

Fill a cocktail shaker with ice. Add the Scotch, honey, Lillet, and lemon juice and shake vigorously. Strain into a chilled martini glass, garnish with the lavender sprig, and serve.

scottish margarita

Look for a single-malt Scotch to add its distinctive character to this drink. Renowned for its peaty, smoky style, Ardbeg, from a distillery on the island of Islay, is Eleven Madison Park's top choice for this twist on the lemon-lime favorite.

Moisten the outside edge of a rocks glass with the lime wedge. Sprinkle a little sea salt on a small plate and dip the moistened rim in the salt to coat it lightly. Fill the glass and a cocktail shaker with ice. Add the Scotch, Cointreau, and lemon, lime, and tangerine juices to the shaker and shake vigorously. Strain into the prepared glass and serve.

1 lime wedge and coarse sea salt for rim

Ice

2 oz single-malt Scotch, preferably Ardbeg

1 oz Cointreau or other orange liqueur

½ oz fresh lemon juice

½ oz fresh lime juice

Splash of fresh tangerine juice

MAKES 1 DRINK

> **"** Our menus are seasonal so we use plenty of fresh fruits and herbs, like lavender, in our cocktails during spring and summer. In fall and winter, we might incorporate pumpkin, quince, pear, and apple flavors. **"**
>
> ELEVEN MADISON PARK BARTENDER

lemon thyme margarita

In this delicate drink from Eleven Madison Park, the pairing of elderflower and lemon thyme produces a refined floral take on the standard favorite. This is a classic martini drinker's margarita.

Fill a cocktail shaker with ice. Add the tequila, elderflower liqueur, lemon thyme syrup, and lime juice and shake vigorously. Strain into a chilled martini glass, garnish with the lemon thyme sprig, and serve.

Ice

1½ oz silver tequila, preferably Herradura

¼ oz St-Germain elderflower liqueur

¾ oz Lemon Thyme Syrup (page 215)

½ oz fresh lime juice

1 sprig fresh lemon thyme

MAKES 1 DRINK

> **"** Build a drink in the glass part of the shaker so everyone can see exactly what's going into the cocktail. **"** GRAMERCY TAVERN BARTENDER

velvet underground

The exotic palate of flavors makes this simple beach sipper a deliciously rich and appealing cocktail, especially when garnished with edible flowers.

Ice	Fill a rocks glass and a cocktail shaker with ice. Add the tequila, Velvet Falernum, passion fruit purée, lime juice, and simple syrup, if desired, to the shaker and shake vigorously. Strain into the glass. Garnish with fresh flower petals, if desired, and serve.
1½ oz silver tequila, preferably Herradura	
1 oz Velvet Falernum (clove-spiced liqueur)	
1 oz Passion Fruit Purée, homemade (page 218) or purchased	
½ oz fresh lime juice	
Splash of Simple Syrup (page 214) (optional)	
Pansy, nasturtium, or other edible flower petals (optional)	

MAKES 1 DRINK

> **"** Any old-time bartender will tell you larger ice cubes are better. And the silicone molds for one-inch cubes are fantastic. **"**

UNION SQUARE CAFE BARTENDER

spirit of agave

Chef Daniel Humm of Eleven Madison Park often presents variations on a single ingredient. Inspired by that tradition, the bartenders created this cocktail, which features agave in three forms: pure nectar, traditional tequila, and smoky mezcal. For extra visual appeal, freeze the lime wheel inside of a large "monster" ice cube.

Fill a cocktail shaker with ice and place the monster ice cube in a rocks glass. Add the tequila, mezcal, Lillet, lime juice, and agave nectar to the shaker and shake vigorously. Strain into the glass. Garnish with the lime wheel, if using, and serve.

Ice, plus 1 monster ice cube

1 oz silver tequila

½ oz *reposado* mezcal

½ oz Lillet Blanc

½ oz fresh lime juice

½ oz agave nectar

1 lime wheel (optional)

MAKES 1 DRINK

BLUE SMOKE

PATRON REPOS
PATRON ANEJO
SAUZA SILVER
SAUZA HORNITOS

WHISKEY

OLD FORESTER
OLD GRANDDAD
OLD OVERHOLT
OLD WHISKEY RIVER
OLD WELLER
VAN WINKLE 12,20 & 23
REBEL YELL
ROCKHILL FARMS
WILD TURKEY RYE
WILD TURKEY 80
WILD TURKEY 101
WILD TURKEY RARE
W L WELLER
WOODFORD RESERVE
WT RUSSELLS RESERVE

COCKTAILS

MINT JULEP
LYNCHBURG LEMONADE
OLD FASHIONED
SAZERAC
SIDECAR
ILLINOIS SWING
PORCH SWING
HAYRIDE
DIRTY RITE
CAIPIRINHA
DARK N STORMY
CLASSIC MARGARITA
BLOOD
CO

SEASONAL   HARPO
SIERRA PALE   ABITA L
HENNEPIN   BUDWEI
BLUEPOINT TOASTED L

SNACKS

BBQ CHIPS   SALT PEA
CHIPOTLE WINGS   DEVILLE
FRY BREAD   CHEESE F
HUSH PUPPIES   PEEL N EA

TRY BLUE SMOKE CATE

LIVE LONGER
DRINK BLUE SMOKE BOU

TOASTED LAGER

BLUE POINT

BLUE SMOKE
ORIGINAL
ALE

casual libations

Some cocktails are casual to the core. Beach favorites like margaritas, daiquiris, and mojitos come to mind. They are the embodiment of fun, friends, and festivity, of afternoon barbecues and alfresco dance parties, of sizzling days and balmy nights.

These refreshing and delicious drinks, enlivened with unusual or seasonal flavors, make for easy entertaining anytime.

contents

coltrane's resolution

This cocktail is Jazz Standard's tribute to "Resolution," one of John Coltrane's best-known tracks from the 1965 album *Love Supreme*, which he called a spiritual search for purity.

Combine the Lillet and blood orange purée in a chilled flute. Fill with the Champagne, garnish with the blood orange slice, if desired, and serve.

1 oz Lillet Blanc

Splash of Blood Orange Purée, homemade (page 218) or purchased

About 5 oz Champagne, chilled

Blood orange slice for garnish (optional)

MAKES 1 DRINK

sparkling campari cocktail

For many years, this easy-to-drink cocktail was a Gramercy Tavern staple. While it's no longer listed on the menu, the bartenders will happily mix it up for anyone who asks.

Fill a flute with crushed ice and a cocktail shaker with ice cubes. Add the Campari mix and grapefruit juice to the shaker and shake vigorously. Strain into the flute and top with the Moscato. Garnish with the candied grapefruit peel and serve.

campari cocktail mix In a large glass jar, combine the Campari, vodka, and vermouth. Add the grapefruit juice and the rind to the jar. Refrigerate for at least 24 hours, then remove the grapefruit rind. The mix will keep, tightly covered in the refrigerator, for up to 1 week.

Crushed ice and ice cubes

6 oz Campari Cocktail Mix (recipe follows)

Splash of fresh grapefruit juice

Splash of Moscato d'Asti

Candied grapefruit peel for garnish

MAKES 1 DRINK

CAMPARI COCKTAIL MIX

1 bottle (1 l) Campari

8 oz vodka

4 oz sweet vermouth

Juice and rind from ½ grapefruit

MAKES ABOUT 1½ QUARTS, OR ENOUGH FOR 8 DRINKS

mutu

Vernaccia is a white wine made most famously in the area around San Gimignano, in Tuscany. Aromatic elderflower liqueur and bright-tasting limoncello complement its crisp, citrusy character in this Italian-inspired cocktail named after Florence soccer star Adrian Mutu.

Fill a Collins glass with ice. Add the Vernaccia, elderflower liqueur, and limoncello. Top with soda water and stir. Garnish with mint leaves and serve.

Ice

About 3 oz Vernaccia or other crisp, white wine

1 oz St-Germain elderflower liqueur

½ oz limoncello, homemade (page 84) or purchased

Soda water to taste

Fresh mint leaves for garnish

MAKES 1 DRINK

CASUAL LIBATIONS

the porch swing

Ice

1½ oz gin, preferably Hendrick's

1½ oz Pimm's No. 1

4 oz Blue Smoke lemonade (see note)

5 thin slices cucumber, cut into 10 half-moons

Splash of 7-Up or lemon soda

MAKES 1 DRINK

This pleasing summertime drink goes down easy. It's a staff and guest favorite, not to mention the 2007 winner of New York City's 2nd Annual Sidewalk Café Drink Mix-Off. To make lemonade the Blue Smoke way, mix together 2 parts freshly squeezed lemon juice, 2 parts water, and 1 part Simple Syrup (page 214). Use immediately.

Fill a Collins glass and a cocktail shaker with ice. Add the gin, Pimm's No. 1, and lemonade to the shaker and shake vigorously. Strain into the glass. Add the cucumber half-moons, top with the 7-Up, and serve.

66 My grandfather is the inspiration behind this combination of Pimm's, cucumber, and gin. As a child, I would sit with him on the back porch of his house in the Catskills and drink lemonade while he drank gin and tonics. 99

BLUE SMOKE BARTENDER

> **66** The importance of using fresh ingredients in the kitchen must translate to the bar. Think farm fresh and seasonal and try to incorporate these same principles into your drinks. **99**
>
> BLUE SMOKE BARTENDER

summer sangria

6 cups full-bodied dry wine such as Merlot or Chardonnay

2 cups Simple Syrup (page 214)

1 cup fresh orange juice

1 cup fresh or unsweetened canned pineapple juice

3 oz white rum, preferably Bacardi

3 oz gin

1 oz triple sec or other orange liqueur

1 oz brandy

Ice

3–3½ cups chopped fresh seasonal fruit

MAKES ABOUT 3 QUARTS, OR ENOUGH FOR 12–14 DRINKS

Hudson Yards makes this cooling sangria with red or white wine, depending on what fruit is freshest in the market. Pair berries and plums with red, or peaches and melons with white. Citrus fruits add balance to both.

Combine the wine, simple syrup, orange and pineapple juices, rum, gin, triple sec, and brandy in a large glass pitcher. Cover and refrigerate for at least 12 hours or up to 24 hours. Fill wine glasses with ice and arrange ¼ cup of the chopped fruit in each. Pour the sangria into the glasses and serve.

161

CASUAL LIBATIONS

> 66 The part of home bartending that is the most fun is finding new ingredients. Every discovery opens up a whole world of options. 99
>
> TABLA BARTENDER

kumquat mojito

The vibrant color and flavor of kumquats make this drink a winter hit. A candied kumquat, or a tiny slice of a fresh one, is an elegant and edible garnish.

Muddle the kumquats and mint leaves in a cocktail shaker. Add ice and the rum, lime juice, and simple syrup and shake vigorously. Pour the contents, including the fruit and mint, into a Collins glass and serve.

2½ kumquats, halved

8 fresh mint leaves

Ice

2 oz white rum, preferably Myers's

1 oz fresh lime juice

1 oz Simple Syrup (page 214)

MAKES 1 DRINK

strawberry-ginger mojito

Ice

2 oz white rum

2 oz Strawberry Purée, homemade (page 218) or purchased

¼ oz Simple Syrup (page 214)

¼ oz fresh or bottled ginger juice

¼ oz fresh lime juice

¼ oz fresh lemon juice

Fresh strawberry for garnish

1 sprig fresh mint (optional)

MAKES 1 DRINK

Bottled ginger juice can be found in well-stocked markets and natural-food stores. To make your own, peel and grate 3 ounces of fresh ginger, wrap in cheesecloth, and tightly twist both ends to squeeze out the juice.

Fill a double rocks glass and a cocktail shaker with ice. Add the rum, strawberry purée, simple syrup, and ginger, lime, and lemon juices to the shaker and shake vigorously. Strain into the glass, garnish with the strawberry and mint sprig, if desired, and serve.

winter mojito

This seasonal cocktail uses the same "drunken cranberries" that made Gramercy Tavern's Cranberry Daiquiri (page 73) a huge hit. The dark rum continues the cool weather theme.

Fill a rocks glass with ice cubes. Muddle 1 teaspoon of the drunken cranberries and the 2 teaspoons of liquid, the lime wedges, and the mint sprigs in a cocktail shaker. Add the rum and crushed ice and shake vigorously. Strain into the glass and top with soda water. Garnish the drink with a few mint leaves and the remaining teaspoon of drunken cranberries and serve.

Ice cubes and crushed ice

2 teaspoons Drunken Cranberries (page 219), plus 2 teaspoons of their liquid

2 lime wedges

8 sprigs fresh mint, plus mint leaves for garnish

2½ oz dark rum, preferably Gosling's

Soda water to taste

MAKES 1 DRINK

watermelon mojito

Choose the juiciest watermelon you can find for this summer-in-a-glass cocktail. To dress it up, garnish the glass with a melon wedge briefly seared on a hot grill.

Fill a double rocks glass with ice. Muddle the watermelon and mint leaves in a cocktail shaker. Add ice and the lime juice, simple syrup, and rum and shake vigorously. Strain into the glass and top with soda water. Garnish with the mint sprigs and serve.

Ice

Four 1-inch cubes fresh watermelon

6 fresh mint leaves, plus mint sprigs for garnish

½ oz fresh lime juice

½ oz Simple Syrup (page 214)

2½ oz white rum

Soda water to taste

MAKES 1 DRINK

the hampton jitney

Named for the eponymous luxury bus that has been carrying city folks to the Hamptons year-round since 1974, this spicy, hip tropical cocktail is perfect for the beach—or for capturing the spirit of it.

Moisten the outside edge of a chilled martini glass with the lemon wedge. Sprinkle a little sugar on a small plate and dip the moistened rim in the sugar to coat it lightly. Fill a cocktail shaker with ice. Add the rum, spiced syrup, and lemon and pineapple juices and shake vigorously. Strain into the glass, garnish with the pineapple slice, and serve.

spiced island syrup In a saucepan, bring the water to a boil over medium heat. Remove from the heat and add the sugar, star anise, clove, cinnamon stick, and vanilla bean, stirring to dissolve the sugar. Let cool to room temperature and then let stand, refrigerated, for 24–36 hours. Strain into a clean glass jar. The syrup will keep, tightly covered in the refrigerator, for up to 3 weeks.

1 lemon wedge and sugar for rim

Ice

1 oz white rum

¾ oz Spiced Island Syrup (recipe follows)

¾ oz fresh lemon juice

¾ oz pineapple juice

1 pineapple slice

MAKES 1 DRINK

SPICED ISLAND SYRUP

1 cup water

1 cup sugar

3 whole star anise pods

1 whole clove

½ cinnamon stick

½ vanilla bean, split lengthwise

MAKES ABOUT 1 CUP,
OR ENOUGH FOR 10 DRINKS

blue smoke lynchburg lemonade

People know to order this traditional Tennessee cooler at Blue Smoke without even looking at the menu. Pair it with Memphis-style baby back ribs and you'll have guests asking for another round. The drink was popularized by Jack Daniel's, but this version triples the whiskey content.

Fill a cocktail shaker and a rocks glass with ice. Add the whiskey, triple sec, and lemonade to the shaker and shake vigorously. Strain into the glass, garnish with the lemon wedge, and serve.

Ice

1½ oz whiskey, preferably Jack Daniel's

½ oz triple sec or other orange liqueur

2 oz Blue Smoke Lemonade (page 158)

1 lemon wedge

MAKES 1 DRINK

the hayride

This Blue Smoke bourbon drink is a fall favorite. It also makes a decadent (grown-up) dessert when swizzled or blended with vanilla ice cream, and the spiced cider can easily stand on its own for a nonalcoholic offering.

Moisten the outside edge of a martini glass with the lemon wedge. Sprinkle a little cinnamon sugar on a small plate and dip the moistened rim in the sugar to coat it lightly. Fill a cocktail shaker with ice. Add the bourbon, pear brandy, and spiced cider and shake vigorously. Strain into the prepared glass, garnish with the pear slice, and serve.

blue smoke spiced cider In a large pot, combine the apple cider, clove-studded orange, cinnamon stick, and allspice berries and bring to a boil over medium heat. Reduce the heat to maintain a gentle simmer and cook until the liquid is reduced by two-thirds, about 30 minutes. Remove from the heat and let cool slightly. Strain into a 1-quart glass bottle and refrigerate. The spiced cider will keep, tightly covered in the refrigerator, for up to 2 weeks.

1 lemon wedge and Cinnamon Sugar (page 217) for rim

Ice

2 oz bourbon, preferably Basil Hayden's

½ oz pear brandy, preferably Carneros Alambic Pear de Pear

2 oz Blue Smoke Spiced Cider (recipe follows)

Fresh or candied pear slice for garnish

MAKES 1 DRINK

BLUE SMOKE SPICED CIDER

3 quarts apple cider

1 small orange, studded with 5 whole cloves

½ cinnamon stick

5 whole allspice berries

MAKES ABOUT 32 OZ, OR ENOUGH FOR 16 DRINKS

CASUAL LIBATIONS

kentucky cream

Blue Smoke uses bourbon instead of whiskey in this Irish cream-inspired cocktail. For a Kentucky Coffee, pour this recipe into freshly brewed coffee and top with whipped cream and chocolate shavings.

Fill 5 rocks glasses with ice. Combine the bourbon, cream, condensed milk, eggs, chocolate syrup, honey, and almond extract in a bowl and mix with an immersion blender on low speed until smooth. Strain into the rocks glasses and serve.

Ice

6½ oz bourbon, preferably Maker's Mark

8 oz heavy cream

4 oz sweetened condensed milk

2 large eggs

1 tablespoon chocolate syrup

1 tablespoon honey

⅛ teaspoon almond extract

MAKES 5 DRINKS

drunken affogato

Many people associate the Italian term *affogato* with espresso, but it literally means "drowned." Hence, its use in this creamy concoction, which is best prepared tableside.

Stir together the Lauria Alpine Cream Liqueur and Calvados in a small pitcher. Scoop the ice cream into a double rocks glass. Using a pastry bag fitted with a plain ½-inch tip, pipe the whipped cream up one side of the glass (this can also be done carefully with a long spoon). Pour the liqueurs over the whipped cream and serve with a parfait spoon.

1½ oz Lauria Alpine Cream Liqueur (pear cream liqueur)

½ oz Calvados or other apple brandy

1 scoop (about ⅓ cup) vanilla ice cream

2 tablespoons whipped cream

MAKES 1 DRINK

> **66** One of the most important tools in your bar should be your library. The more you know about what other bartenders have done, the more successful your own creativity will be. **99**

TABLA BARTENDER

run for the roses

Created for a Kentucky Derby party, this distinctive julep uses turbinado sugar for an earthy mint syrup that gives the bourbon a rich voice.

Fill a Collins glass or silver mint julep cup with crushed ice. Add the mint syrup and bourbon; if using a mint julep cup, stir briskly with a bar spoon until the cup is frosty. Garnish with the mint sprig and a straw and serve.

Crushed ice

1 oz Mint Syrup (page 215)

1½ oz bourbon, preferably Maker's Mark

1 sprig fresh mint

MAKES 1 DRINK

blood orange margarita

1 lime wedge and coarse salt, preferably Maldon, for rim

Ice

2 oz tequila, preferably Sauza Hornitos

1½ oz fresh lime juice

¾ oz orange liqueur, preferably GranGala

½ oz Simple Syrup (page 214)

¾ oz Blood Orange Purée, homemade (page 218) or purchased

1 lime wheel

1 blood orange wheel (optional)

MAKES 1 DRINK

For seven years running, this citrusy blend, juiced up with GranGala orange liqueur, has been Blue Smoke's most popular cocktail.

Moisten the outside edge of a rocks glass with the lime wedge. Sprinkle a little salt on a small plate and dip the moistened rim in the salt to coat it lightly. Fill the glass and a cocktail shaker with ice. Add the tequila, lime juice, orange liqueur, simple syrup, and blood orange purée to the shaker and shake vigorously. Strain into the glass, garnish with the lime wheel and the blood orange wheel, if desired, and serve.

watermelon margarita

Charred lemon slices make a sophisticated garnish for this distinctly summer margarita. They are easy to make: cut a lemon into slices ⅛ inch thick, dredge the slices in turbinado sugar, and sear with a kitchen torch.

Fill a rocks glass and a cocktail shaker with ice. Add the tequila, lime juice, watermelon purée, elderflower liqueur, and simple syrup to the shaker and shake vigorously. Strain into the glass, garnish with charred lemon, if desired, and serve.

Ice

2 oz *reposado* tequila, preferably Patrón

1½ oz fresh lime juice

1 oz Watermelon Purée, homemade (page 218) or purchased

½ oz St-Germain elderflower liqueur

½ oz Simple Syrup (page 214)

Charred lemon (see note) or lemon wedges for garnish (optional)

MAKES 1 DRINK

hard thyme lemonade

This not-too-strong sipper adds the dusky herbal notes of thyme to bright lemon for a perfect garden drink. A fresh thyme variety with variegated leaves, such as silver thyme, makes a striking garnish.

Fill a cocktail shaker and a double rocks glass with ice. Add the water, lemon juice, thyme syrup, and vodka to the shaker and shake vigorously. Strain into the glass, garnish with the thyme sprig, and serve.

Ice

2 oz water

1 oz fresh lemon juice

1 oz Thyme Syrup
(page 215)

1½ oz vodka

1 sprig fresh thyme

MAKES 1 DRINK

dirty pete

Ice

2½ oz vodka,
preferably Ketel One

1½ oz Spanish Queen olive brine

5 or 6 dashes of hot-pepper sauce,
preferably Texas Pete

2 pitted Spanish Queen olives

1 pickled jalapeño

MAKES 1 DRINK

Danny Meyer helped create this spunky cross between a dirty martini and a Bloody Mary for Blue Smoke. Texas Pete hot sauce and a jalapeño garnish deliver the spicy kick.

Fill a cocktail shaker and a rocks glass with ice. Add the vodka, olive brine, and hot-pepper sauce to the shaker and shake vigorously. Strain into the glass, garnish with the olives and pickled jalapeño, and serve.

spiked arnold palmer

Ice

2 cups vodka, preferably Finlandia

4¾ cups freshly brewed tea, chilled

3 cups water

1 cup Lemon Syrup (page 215)

¾ cup fresh lemon juice

10 sprigs fresh mint

MAKES ABOUT 3 QUARTS,
OR ENOUGH FOR 10 DRINKS

If Shake Shack served spirits beyond beer and wine, this would be on the menu. The classic nonalcoholic version is always offered, but the staff adds vodka when they serve it at home. You can also substitute mint syrup for the lemon.

Fill 10 highball glasses with ice. Combine the vodka, tea, water, lemon syrup, and lemon juice in a large pitcher and stir to mix well. Pour into the glasses, garnish each with a mint sprig, and serve.

183

love for sale

Ice

1½ oz mandarin-flavored vodka,
preferably Absolut Mandrin

1 oz Passoã (passion fruit liqueur)

1 oz fresh orange juice

1 oz pineapple juice

Squeeze of fresh lime juice

1 orange wheel

MAKES 1 DRINK

Reminiscent of a Cosmopolitan, this smooth, fruity drink featuring passion fruit liqueur was named after a famous Cole Porter song and made its debut at Jazz Standard.

Fill a cocktail shaker with ice. Add the vodka, Passoã, and orange, pineapple, and lime juices and shake vigorously. Strain into a chilled martini glass, garnish with the orange wheel, and serve.

bar fare

Cocktail-friendly foods should complement the flavor profiles of the drinks they accompany. The clean flavors of fresh seafood, like ceviche or grilled shrimp, are good matches for citrus-driven cocktails. Bold-flavored bourbon- or rye-based drinks pair well with bites substantial enough to hold their own against their brassy partners. Of course the popular, time-tested bar snacks—nuts, popcorn, chips, and olives—pair well with nearly every cocktail.

contents

gramercy tavern bar nuts

The balance of salty, sweet, and spicy makes these nuts irresistible—no wonder Pastry Chef Nancy Olson makes them by the gallon. They're a great complement to nearly any cocktail, but pair especially well with the Ginger Tonic (page 62) or Cranberry Daiquiri (page 73).

To make the spice mix, in a small bowl, stir together the sugar, salts, cumin, cinnamon, cayenne, ginger, black pepper, and nutmeg. Set aside.

Preheat the oven to 300°F. Spread the almonds on a rimmed baking sheet and bake until lightly toasted, about 10 minutes. Immediately transfer to a plate and let cool. Reduce the oven temperature to 275°F and grease a clean rimmed baking sheet with the grapeseed oil.

In a large bowl, combine the almonds, pecans, cashews, simple syrup, corn syrup, the 1 tablespoon grapeseed oil, and the spice mix. Toss gently until the nuts are evenly coated. Spread on the prepared baking sheet.

Bake until the spice mixture is caramelized and the nuts are lightly toasted, 25–40 minutes. (To check for doneness, take a few nuts out of the oven and let cool for a few minutes; if done, they will be dry to the touch.) Let cool completely. Store in an airtight container in a cool, dark place for up to 1 week.

SPICE MIX

3 tablespoons turbinado sugar

1 tablespoon kosher salt

1¼ teaspoons table salt

2¼ teaspoons ground cumin

1 teaspoon ground cinnamon

1 teaspoon cayenne pepper

¾ teaspoon ground ginger

½ teaspoon freshly ground black pepper

¼ teaspoon freshly grated nutmeg

1 cup almonds

1 tablespoon grapeseed oil, plus more for greasing

2 cups pecan halves

1¼ cups cashews

2 oz Simple Syrup (page 214)

1½ teaspoons light corn syrup

MAKES ABOUT 4 CUPS

five-spice cashews

Dry-toasting spices until they pop adds a smoky edge to crunchy, buttery cashews. Seek out Sichuan peppercorns at Asian stores, spice markets, or online. Take a cue from Hudson Yards and serve this versatile snack while mixing drinks to order at a cocktail paty.

To make the spice mix, in a small, dry frying pan over high heat, toast the fennel seeds, star anise, Sichuan peppercorns, cloves, and white, pink, and black peppercorns, shaking the pan constantly, until they smoke and the peppercorns start to pop, about 5 minutes. Let cool. Transfer to a spice grinder or a clean coffee grinder and process to a fine powder. Pour into a bowl and stir in the salt, cinnamon, ginger, and cayenne.

In a large saucepan over high heat, combine the cashews, sugars, and water. Cook, stirring often, until the sugars have dissolved completely and the sugar syrup begins to thicken, about 6–8 minutes. At this point, stir constantly until the sugar crystallizes and is sandy, 3–5 minutes longer.

Add the spice mix and continue to cook, stirring constantly, until the sugar just begins to re-melt, about 1 minute longer. Pour onto a baking sheet and let cool.

Toss the nuts in a fine-mesh sieve to remove any extra spice dust before serving. Store in an airtight container at room temperature for up to 2 weeks.

CASHEW SPICE MIX

1 tablespoon plus 1 teaspoon fennel seeds

5 star anise pods

1 tablespoon plus 1 teaspoon Sichuan peppercorns

2 teaspoons whole cloves

2 teaspoons white peppercorns

2 teaspoons pink peppercorns

2 teaspoons black peppercorns

2 teaspoons kosher salt

2 teaspoons ground cinnamon

2 teaspoons ground ginger

1 teaspoon cayenne pepper

1 lb unsalted roasted cashews

¾ cup granulated sugar

¾ cup lightly packed brown sugar

¼ cup water

MAKES ABOUT 5 CUPS

dried cherry, bacon, and pecan mix

Dubbed "The Holiday Mix," this lavish and addictive bar snack became a most-requested item at Hudson Yards holiday parties after it was introduced last year.

To make the candied bacon, preheat the oven to 350°F. Lay the bacon on a rimmed baking sheet and bake, rotating the pan after 10 minutes, until the bacon starts to crisp, about 15 minutes. Drain off any fat from the pan. In a small bowl, stir together the brown sugar, cayenne, and cloves. Sprinkle the sugar mixture on the bacon, return to the oven, and bake until the bacon is very crisp and the sugar mixture is bubbling, about 5 minutes. Transfer the bacon to a cutting board and let cool. Leave the oven on.

In a saucepan over high heat, combine ½ lb of the pecans, the granulated sugar, and the water. Cook, stirring often, until the sugar melts and thickens to a syrup, 6–8 minutes. At this point, stir constantly until the syrup crystallizes and is sandy, 3–5 minutes longer. Pour onto a baking sheet and let cool.

In a bowl, stir together the egg white, salt, and cloves. Add the reminaing ½ lb pecans, toss to coat, and spread on a rimmed baking sheet. Bake until lightly toasted, about 5 minutes. Let cool.

Cut the bacon into ½-inch pieces. In a bowl, toss together the bacon, praline, toasted pecans, cherries, and orange peel and serve. The nut mix, without bacon, can be stored in an airtight container at room temperature for up to 1 week.

CANDIED BACON

3 slices thick-cut applewood or other wood-smoked bacon

¼ cup lightly packed dark brown sugar

1 teaspoon cayenne pepper

½ teaspoon ground cloves

1 lb pecan pieces

1 cup granulated sugar

½ cup water

1 large egg white, lightly beaten

1½ teaspoons kosher salt

¼ teaspoon ground cloves

½ cup dried cherries or dried cranberries

¼ cup chopped candied orange peel

MAKES ABOUT 5 CUPS

union square cafe bar nuts

¼ lb *each* peeled peanuts, cashews, Brazil nuts, hazelnuts, walnuts, pecans, and unpeeled almonds, or 1¼ lb unsalted assorted nuts

2 tablespoons coarsely chopped fresh rosemary

2 teaspoons dark brown sugar

2 teaspoons kosher salt

½ teaspoon cayenne pepper

1 tablespoon unsalted butter, melted

MAKES 5 CUPS

Every afternoon just before five, a piping-hot batch of this nut mix emerges from the kitchen at Union Square Cafe and makes its way to the bar. The sweet rosemary fragrance has been irresistible to guests for more than 20 years. Any Favorite Classic cocktail (page 20) would pair perfectly.

Preheat the oven to 350°F.

Combine the nuts in a large bowl and toss to mix well. Spread in a single layer on a rimmed baking sheet. Toast in the oven, stirring once or twice, until light golden brown, about 10 minutes.

In the same bowl, stir together the rosemary, brown sugar, salt, cayenne, and melted butter. Add the warm nuts and toss to coat thoroughly. Serve warm. Store in an airtight container at room temperature for up to 1 week.

tamarind-spiced pistachios

Chaat masala, a spice blend used to flavor an assortment of Indian snacks, gets its distinctive flavor from sulfurous black salt. Look for it in Indian markets. At Tabla, Chef Floyd Cardoz uses unshelled pistachios for more interactive snacking. They're delicious served alongside the CP Daiquiri (page 99) or Tablatini (page 100).

(page 99) or Tablatini (page 100).

Preheat the oven to 350°F.

In a cast iron or other ovenproof skillet over medium heat, melt the butter. When the butter just begins to brown, add the curry leaves, rosemary, and ginger and cook, stirring occasionaly, until fragrant, about 3–4 minutes. Add the salt, cayenne, Aleppo and black peppers, mustard, brown sugar, *chaat masala*, pomegranate seeds, and cumin and cook for 2–3 minutes longer. Add the tamarind and cook for 5–7 minutes longer. Add the pistachios and stir to coat.

Transfer the skillet to the oven and bake until dry, about 10 minutes. Let cool. Store in an airtight container at room temperature for up to 3 weeks.

1½ tablespoons unsalted butter

2 fresh curry leaves

½ sprig fresh rosemary

1½ teaspoons ground ginger

1 teaspoon kosher salt

⅛ teaspoon cayenne pepper

¼ teaspoon Aleppo pepper, or ⅛ teaspoon more cayenne pepper

⅛ teaspoon freshly ground black pepper

⅛ teaspoon dry mustard

⅛ teaspoon brown sugar

½ teaspoon *chaat masala*, preferably MDH brand

1 tablespoon dried pomegranate seeds, finely ground

¼ teaspoon cumin seeds, finely ground

3 tablespoons tamarind powder

½ lb unsalted pistachios

MAKES ABOUT 1½ CUPS

thai trail mix

1 cup unsalted raw cashews

1 cup shelled unsalted peanuts

2 tablespoons kosher salt

⅛ teaspoon cayenne pepper

½ cup toasted unsweetened dried coconut shards (see note)

½ cup dried papaya

½ cup dried mango

½ cup dried banana chips

MAKES ABOUT 4 CUPS

Dried coconut flakes, or "shards," are available in bulk at natural-food stores. To toast, spread them on a baking sheet and bake at 350°F just until golden, 3–4 minutes. A nice late-afternoon snack, this Hudson Yards creation pairs well with the Thai Basil Bliss (page 88) or any margarita.

Preheat the oven to 350°F.

Spread the cashews on a rimmed baking sheet and toast until lightly golden, about 7 minutes. Meanwhile, spread the peanuts on a rimmed baking sheet and toast until lightly golden, about 5 minutes. Pour the hot nuts into a large bowl and add the salt and cayenne. Toss to mix well.

Add the coconut, papaya, and mango and stir to mix well. Let cool completely, then add the banana chips and serve. Store in an airtight container at room temperature for up to 2 weeks.

blue smoke devilled eggs

Few can turn down a devilled egg, and Blue Smoke's mustardy, slightly piquant version is a straight-up classic. Pass a platter at your next barbecue or game-day party to please the crowd, especially the beer or bourbon drinkers.

Place the eggs in a large saucepan of cold, salted water. Place over high heat and bring to a boil. Immediately reduce the heat to maintain a simmer and cook for exactly 9 minutes. Using a slotted spoon, remove the eggs from the water and place under cold running water until cool to the touch. Gently crack the shells and peel the eggs under the running water.

Halve the eggs. Scoop the yolks into a food processor and process until smooth. Cut a thin slice from the underside of each white, so they will sit flat on a plate; arrange them on a plate and set aside. Add the mayonnaise, vinegar, Dijon and dry mustards, cayenne, and curry powder, if using, to the yolks. Process briefly until well combined. Taste and adjust the seasoning with salt and black pepper.

Spoon the yolk mixture into a pastry bag fitted with a large star tip. Pipe the mixture into the egg whites. Garnish with the paprika, if using, and serve immediately, or cover and refrigerate for up to 2 days.

10 large eggs

7 tablespoons good-quality mayonnaise such as Hellman's or Best Foods

1 teaspoon Champagne vinegar

2 teaspoons Dijon mustard

½ teaspoon dry mustard such as Coleman's

¼ teaspoon cayenne pepper

¼ teaspoon curry powder (optional)

Kosher salt and freshly ground black pepper

¼ teaspoon paprika (optional)

MAKES 6–8 SERVINGS

fried green olives

Lightly coating olives with a crunchy crust and deep-frying them heightens their savory appeal. Hudson Yards serves this salty snack frequently as it complements nearly any cocktail they pour.

Line a rimmed baking sheet with parchment paper and set aside. Place the olives in a colander and shake to remove excess moisture. Place the *panko* in a food processor and pulse a few times until processed to a medium-fine consistency. Pour into a small bowl. Place the flour in another bowl and the eggs in a third bowl; beat the eggs lightly to blend.

Place 10 olives in the flour and roll to coat completely; shake off the excess flour. Place the olives in the bowl with the eggs, coat completely, and remove with a slotted spoon, letting the excess egg drain off. Place the olives in the bowl with the *panko* and shake the bowl to coat completely. Using a clean slotted spoon, transfer the coated olives to the prepared baking sheet. Repeat to coat the remaining olives. Place the baking sheet in the freezer for 1 hour.

Pour oil into a large, heavy-bottomed, straight-sided pan, 8–10 inches wide, to a depth of 1¼ inches. The pan should be no more than one-fourth full to prevent any bubbling over when frying the olives. Heat the oil until it registers 350°F on a deep-frying thermometer. Working in batches, gently lower 15 olives into the oil and fry until golden brown, about 5 minutes. Using a slotted spoon, transfer to a paper towel–lined plate to drain briefly. Repeat 3 times to fry the remaining olives, letting the oil return to 350°F between batches. Serve at once.

BAR FARE

60 pitted green olives
(about 2 cups)

2½ cups *panko*
(Japanese bread crumbs)

1 cup all-purpose flour

2 large eggs

Vegetable oil for frying

SERVES 6–8

marinated olives

1 tablespoon fennel seeds

1 lb brine-packed olives such as Gaeta, Niçoise, or Picholine

1 cup extra-virgin olive oil

3 cloves garlic, peeled and flattened with the flat side of a knife blade

1 tablespoon red pepper flakes

Zest of 1 orange, cut into thin strips

SERVES 8–12

For years, Union Square Cafe has greeted its guests with a ramekin of these Roman-style marinated olives. They pair well with most cocktails, making them an ideal choice for parties, but are particularly enlivened by aperitif-style drinks like A Fino Introduction (page 122).

In a small, dry frying pan over medium heat, toast the fennel seeds, shaking the pan constantly, until lightly browned and fragrant, 2–3 minutes. Immediately transfer to a plate and let cool.

Drain the olives, place them in a bowl, and rinse in several changes of cold water until the water runs clear. Pour the olives into a colander, drain well, and shake to remove excess water.

In a large, clean jar, combine the olives, oil, garlic, red pepper flakes, orange zest, and fennel seeds. Cover tightly and shake well. Marinate at room temperature for 3–5 hours before serving. Store in the refrigerator for up to 1 month.

> **"** Know your guests. Each bar snack fits a different type of party and helps generate conversation and set the tone. Serve items that are unique but won't leave you scrambling. **"**
>
> HUDSON YARDS CHEF

black truffled popcorn

Popcorn goes uptown when tossed with warm black truffle butter and oil. Look for truffle-infused specialty products at gourmet markets. Created by Chef Gabriel Kreuther to serve with cocktails in The Modern's Bar Room, this snack is particularly pleasing with Coming Up Roses (page 120).

In a large pot with a lid over medium heat, heat the grapeseed oil until it shimmers. Add the popcorn, cover, and shake until most of the kernels have popped, 4–5 minutes. Pour into a large bowl.

In a small saucepan over low heat, melt the butter with the truffle oil until warm. Drizzle over the popcorn, season to taste with salt, and serve at once.

2 tablespoons grapeseed oil

½ cup popcorn kernels

3 tablespoons black truffle butter

3 tablespoons black truffle oil

Kosher salt

MAKES ABOUT 12 CUPS

> **"** When you're throwing a large cocktail party, speed is key. Make delicious food that's easy, quickly duplicated, and can sit at room temperature without losing its integrity. **"**
>
> HUDSON YARDS CHEF

citrus popcorn

Popcorn is a surprisingly delicious match with sparkling wine, which is why Hudson Yards created this lemony, buttery version. It also goes well with a Bloody Mary for a fun brunch pairing, setting the tone for a casual gathering.

In a saucepan over medium-low heat, melt the butter. Stir in the lemon zest and juice, 3 tablespoons salt, and the sugar until the salt and sugar are dissolved.

Meanwhile, in a large pot with a lid over medium heat, heat the grapeseed oil until it shimmers. Add the popcorn, cover, and shake until most of the kernels have popped, 4–5 minutes. Pour into a large bowl. Strain the butter mixture through a fine-mesh sieve over the hot popcorn and toss to coat. Taste and adjust the seasoning with salt and pepper and serve at once.

½ lb unsalted butter

Finely grated zest of 1 lemon

⅔ cup fresh lemon juice

Salt and freshly ground pepper

½ tablespoon sugar

1½ tablespoons grapeseed oil

⅓ cup popcorn kernels

MAKES ABOUT 10 CUPS

hot garlic potato chips

3–3½ lb Idaho potatoes, peeled

Vegetable oil for frying

3 tablespoons unsalted butter

1 tablespoon pressed garlic

2 tablespoons chopped fresh flat-leaf (Italian) parsley

1 teaspoon kosher salt

⅛ teaspoon freshly ground pepper

MAKES 6–8 SERVINGS

These addictive chips, served at Union Square Cafe, can be made several hours ahead. Store in an airtight container and reheat at 350°F until hot, about 5 minutes. Toss with the garlic butter just before serving.

Using a mandoline or a sharp knife, slice the potatoes about ¹⁄₁₆ inch thick. You should have about 6 cups. Rinse the potatoes in several changes of cold water until the water runs clear. Spin the slices in a salad spinner, and then pat completely dry with paper towels to prevent oil spatters.

Line 2 baking sheets with paper towels. Pour oil into a large, wide, straight-sided saucepan to a depth of 1½ inches. The pan should be no more than one-fourth full. Heat the oil until it registers 315°F on a deep-frying thermometer, or until a cube of bread dropped into the oil floats to the surface and lightly browns in 2–3 minutes.

Working in batches, fry the potato slices, stirring constantly with a slotted spoon to ensure even cooking, until lightly browned and crisp, 15–20 minutes. (If the slices brown faster, the oil is too hot and they won't be cooked through or crisp.) Using the slotted spoon, transfer the chips to the prepared baking sheets to drain. Let the oil return to 315°F between batches. Keep warm in a low oven until all of the chips are fried, and then place them in a large bowl.

In a small saucepan over medium heat, melt the butter. Stir in the garlic and cook until fragrant but not browned, about 1 minute. Drizzle the garlic butter over the chips, add the parsley, salt, and pepper, and stir gently with a rubber spatula, taking care not to break up the chips. Serve hot.

warm tomato chutney dip

For this year-round recipe that uses canned tomatoes, buy a top-quality organic product, such as Muir brand, recommended by Tabla Chef Floyd Cardoz (for a little extra flavor, try their "fire-roasted" variety). Look for tamarind paste at Asian markets and specialty-food stores.

Working in batches, pulse the strained tomatoes in a food processor until coarsely chopped.

In a large saucepan over medium-high heat, heat the oil until it shimmers. Add the yellow and brown mustard, cumin, and nigella seeds and cook, shaking the pan constantly. When they start to pop, after about 30 seconds, add the onion, ginger, garlic, and chiles. Immediately reduce the heat to medium and cook, stirring, until the onion and garlic have softened but not browned, 2–3 minutes. Stir in a pinch of salt and the tomatoes. Bring the mixture to a boil, then reduce the heat to maintain a very gentle simmer and cook for 1 hour.

Stir in the tamarind paste and sugar. Taste and adjust the seasoning with salt and pepper and remove from the heat. Serve warm or at room temperature, or let cool completely and store in an airtight container in the refrigerator for up to 2 weeks, or freeze for up to 1 month.

2 cans (28 oz each) whole or chopped tomatoes, strained

¼ cup canola oil

1 teaspoon yellow mustard seeds

1 teaspoon brown mustard seeds

1 teaspoon cumin seeds

1 teaspoon nigella seeds

1 white onion, finely chopped

3 tablespoons peeled and minced fresh ginger

2 tablespoons minced garlic

2 small dried red chiles, chopped

Kosher salt and freshly ground pepper

2 tablespoons tamarind paste

1 tablespoon sugar

MAKES ABOUT 4 CUPS

goan guacamole

2½ teaspoons cumin seeds

6 ripe but firm Hass avocados

2 teaspoons grated lime zest

⅓ cup fresh lime juice

½ red onion, finely chopped

1 cup diced plum tomatoes

2 tablespoons chopped
fresh cilantro

¼ cup extra-virgin olive oil

⅛ teaspoon cayenne pepper

Pinch of sugar

Kosher salt and freshly ground
black pepper

Ground cumin for garnish
(optional)

MAKE 6 SERVINGS

This Tabla classic makes the most of the lush texture of avocado. Serve it on its own or with crisp lentil-based *pappadam* (flatbread) alongside. Any cocktail with a bit of heat, such as the Kachumber Kooler (page 94) or Payback (page 87) would be enhanced when served with this inspired version of a bar snack staple.

In a small, dry frying pan over medium heat, toast the cumin seeds, shaking the pan constantly, until they are fragrant and slightly darker, about 3 minutes. Let cool. Transfer to a spice grinder or a clean coffee grinder and process to a coarse powder. Pour into a small bowl and set aside.

Halve and pit the avocados. Scoop out each half, cut the flesh into ½-inch dice, and transfer to a large bowl. Gently toss the avocado with the lime zest and juice and then gently mix in the onion, tomatoes, and cilantro, taking care not to mash the avocados. Mix in the oil, ground cumin seeds, cayenne, and sugar. Taste and adjust the seasoning with salt and pepper. Transfer to a serving bowl and garnish with a pinch of ground cumin, if using. Serve immediately, or place a piece of plastic wrap directly on the surface to prevent browning and refrigerate for up to 2 hours.

crostini with root vegetables and goat cheese

Earthy yet elegant, this Hudson Yards creation balances the natural sweetness of root vegetables with tangy fresh goat cheese. It partners well with a light aperitif, such as the Venetian Spritz (page 30) or Sparkling Campari (page 154).

1 small red beet

1 small parsnip

1 small turnip

1 carrot

1 small celery root

3 tablespoons olive oil

Salt and freshly ground pepper

2 large egg yolks

5 tablespoons sherry vinegar

1½ cups grapeseed oil

2 tablespoons hazelnut oil

1 baguette, cut on the diagonal into 16 thin slices

½ cup fresh goat cheese, at room temperature

Fresh herbs for garnish

Fleur de sel or other sea salt for garnish

MAKES 16 CROSTINI

Preheat the oven to 400°F. Place the beet, parsnip, turnip, carrot, and celery root in a large nonstick roasting pan. Drizzle with 1 tablespoon of the olive oil, season with salt and pepper, and toss to coat. Roast, turning occasionally, until tender when pierced with a knife, 45–50 minutes. Let cool. Reduce the oven temperature to 350°F. Peel and chop the cooled vegetables and then put them in a bowl. Put the beets in a separate bowl (to prevent them from staining the other vegetables). You should have about 2 cups total.

Meanwhile, in a food processor, pulse together the egg yolks and vinegar. With the motor running, add the grapeseed and hazelnut oils in a slow, steady stream and process until smooth. Season with salt and pepper. Pour some of the dressing over the beets and the mixed vegetables and toss to coat lightly. Reserve the remaining dressing for another use.

Arrange the baguette slices on a baking sheet, brush with the remaining olive oil, and season with salt and pepper. Bake until lightly browned and crisp, 8–10 minutes. Let cool, then spread each toast with 2 teaspoons of the cheese. Divide the vegetables evenly among the toasts. Garnish with fresh herbs and *fleur de sel* and serve.

crostini with sweet-pea pesto

This bright green pesto tastes like spring. At Hudson Yards, Chef Robb Garceau also dollops it over delicate capellini and passes it at cocktail parties in small, shallow ramekins.

Preheat the oven to 350°F. Brush the baguette slices lightly with oil and arrange on a baking sheet. Bake until crisp and lightly golden, 8–10 minutes. Set aside.

Meanwhile, bring a saucepan of lightly salted water to a boil. Add the sweet peas and cook for 1 minute. Drain and immerse the sweet peas in ice water to stop the cooking. Drain and set aside.

In a food processor, combine the basil, parsley, 1 cup of the peas, and the garlic. Pulse until the mixture is finely chopped. Taste and adjust the seasoning with salt and pepper. With the motor running, add the ¾ cup olive oil in a slow, steady stream and process until the mixture is smooth.

Top each crostini with the sweet-pea pesto, a few of the remaining peas, and a sprinkling of cheese. Arrange on a platter and serve.

1 baguette, cut on the diagonal into 20 thin slices

¾ cup olive oil, plus oil for brushing

1½ cups shelled fresh sweet peas

4 cups loosely packed fresh basil leaves

2 cups loosely packed fresh flat-leaf (Italian) parsley leaves

1 clove garlic

Sea salt and freshly ground pepper

1 cup grated Parmesan cheese

MAKES 20 CROSTINI

grilled watermelon with heirloom tomatoes

6 large slices seedless watermelon, ¾ inches thick

6 mixed (red, yellow, and green) ripe heirloom tomatoes, sliced

6 tablespoons extra-virgin olive oil

Kosher salt and freshly ground pepper

6 teaspoons aged balsamic vinegar

Sprigs of fresh opal and green basil for garnish

Maldon sea salt for garnish

MAKES 6 SERVINGS

Use a mix of green and opal (purple) basil, available at specialty-produce and farmers' markets, to accentuate the bright colors of this striking summertime salad created by Chef Daniel Humm at Eleven Madison Park. Pair this dish with any refreshing summer cocktail or Champagne drink.

Prepare a charcoal or gas grill for direct grilling over high heat.

Using a 4-inch cookie cutter, cut the watermelon into rounds. Arrange the watermelon rounds on the grate directly over the heat and grill on one side just until grill-marked, 1–2 minutes. Transfer each round, grill-marked side up, to a salad plate.

Place the tomato slices in a large bowl and toss gently with 2 tablespoons of the olive oil. Season to taste with kosher salt and pepper.

Arrange the tomatoes over the watermelon rounds, dividing them evenly. Drizzle the salads with the remaining 4 tablespoons oil and the vinegar. Garnish each salad with the opal or basil sprigs and a sprinkling of sea salt and serve.

red snapper ceviche

Other types of fish are sometimes marketed as snapper, so ask your fishmonger for true red snapper and make sure it's fresh. Popular at Hudson Yards parties, this cool classic is a winning match with The Modern Martini (page 58).

In a small frying pan, heat the oil over high heat. Add the bell pepper and jalapeño and sauté just until seared, about 1 minute. Transfer to a small bowl and refrigerate until cold, at least 30 minutes or up to 12 hours.

Remove any small bones from the snapper fillets. Using a very sharp knife, finely dice the fillets and place in a bowl. Add the red and chile peppers and the juice of 2 of the limes and stir gently. Taste and adjust the seasoning with salt, pepper, lime juice, and simple syrup. Gently stir in the cilantro. Spoon into small bowls. Garnish with the avocado and yucca chips, if desired, and serve.

1 teaspoon vegetable oil

½ cup finely diced red bell pepper

½ jalapeño chile, seeded and finely diced

1 lb red snapper fillets

3 limes

Sea salt and freshly ground white pepper

Splash of Simple Syrup (page 214), or as needed

2 tablespoons chopped fresh cilantro

1 avocado, pitted, peeled, and sliced (optional)

Yucca chips for garnish (optional)

MAKES 6–8 SERVINGS

tequila-lime shrimp

MARINADE

2 tablespoons olive oil

½ red onion, chopped

1 clove garlic, peeled and halved

1 teaspoon chopped seeded
jalapeño chile

½ cup tequila

3 fresh cilantro sprigs,
lightly crushed

2 tablespoons fresh lime juice

PICO DE GALLO

4 plum tomatoes, seeded
and finely diced

½ red onion, finely chopped

1 seeded jalapeño chile, finely diced

Leaves of 3 fresh cilantro
sprigs, chopped

Juice of 1 lime

1 tablespoon olive oil

Salt and freshly ground pepper

1½ lb medium shrimp
(21–25 count), peeled and deveined

20 snow peas, trimmed

MAKES 20 HORS D'OEUVRES

For an elegant presentation, take inspiration from Hudson Yards Chef Robb Garceau and line a serving platter with paper-thin lime wheels. Any margarita is a natural partner.

To make the marinade, in a frying pan, heat 1 tablespoon of the oil over medium-high heat. Add the onion, garlic, and jalapeño and sauté until lightly browned, about 6 minutes. Reduce the heat to medium-low, slowly pour in the tequila, and simmer until the liquid is reduced by one-fourth, about 20 minutes. Pour into a bowl, let cool slightly, and stir in the remaining 1 tablespoon oil and the cilantro and lime juice. Let cool completely.

To make the *pico de gallo*, combine the tomatoes, onion, jalapeño, and cilantro in a bowl and toss gently to mix. Stir in the lime juice and oil. Taste and adjust the seasoning with salt and pepper. Set aside.

Prepare a charcoal or gas grill for direct grilling over medium-high heat. Add the shrimp to the marinade and let stand for 15 minutes. Grill the shrimp, turning once, until opaque throughout, about 2 minutes per side. Let cool.

Meanwhile, bring a saucepan of lightly salted water to a boil. Add the snow peas and cook for 1 minute. Drain and immerse the snow peas in ice water to stop the cooking. Drain and pat dry.

Weave 1 snow pea over the body and under the tail of each shrimp, forming an S shape with the snow pea. Secure the snow pea in place with a cocktail pick. Top each with a spoonful of *pico de gallo* and serve.

simple syrups

A versatile mixer and essential element of many cocktails, simple syrup is a bar staple that can be stored in the refrigerator for up to 2 weeks.

Using the basic recipe as a building block, you can draw on your experience in the kitchen to inspire new flavor combinations in the bar. Add an elegant twist to a martini by shaking a bit of Cardamom Syrup with vodka, or create a spirited Champagne cocktail by first pouring 1–2 oz of Ginger-Lime Syrup into a flute.

Add any of these syrups to iced tea, or mix them with crushed ice and soda to make a refreshing nonalcoholic spritzer. For a dressed-up dessert, drizzle Lavender Syrup and Poire Willliam pear liqueur over vanilla ice cream.

simple syrup

1 cup sugar · 1 cup water

In a saucepan over medium-high heat, combine the sugar and water and bring to a boil, stirring until the sugar is dissolved. Remove from the heat and let cool. Pour into a glass jar, cover, and refrigerate until needed. Makes about 1½ cups.

ginger-honey syrup

1 cup honey · 1 cup water · 3 tablespoons peeled and finely chopped fresh ginger

In a saucepan over medium heat, combine the honey and water and bring to a boil, stirring until the honey is dissolved. Remove from the heat and stir in the ginger. Let cool. Strain into a glass jar, cover, and refrigerate for at least 24 hours or until needed. Makes about 1½ cups.

lavender syrup

1 cup lavender honey · ¾ cup water · 2 teaspoons dried organic lavender (available from tea stores and specialty grocers)

In a saucepan over medium heat, combine the lavender honey and water and warm, stirring to dissolve the honey, until just below the boiling point. Remove from the heat and stir in the lavender. Let stand for 15 minutes. (If the mixture steeps longer, it will become bitter.) Strain into a glass jar and let cool. Cover and refrigerate until needed. Makes about 1¼ cups.

homemade grenadine

⅔ cup pomegranate juice (POM or other high-quality, 100% juice) ¼ cup sugar · ⅓ cup dried hibiscus flowers (available from tea stores and specialty grocers)

In a saucepan over medium heat, combine the pomegranate juice and sugar and bring to a boil, stirring until the sugar is dissolved. Add the dried hibiscus flowers and simmer until the liquid is reduced by half. Remove from the heat and let cool slightly. Strain into a glass jar and let cool. Cover and refrigerate until needed. Makes about ½ cup.

mint syrup

¾ cup turbinado sugar · ¾ cup water · 1 cup chopped fresh mint

In a saucepan over medium-high heat, combine the sugar and water and bring to a boil, stirring until the sugar is dissolved. Remove from the heat and add the fresh mint. Cover and let stand at room temperature for 3–5 hours. Strain into a glass jar, cover, and refrigerate until needed. Makes about 1 cup.

cardamom syrup

**1 cup tupelo (or lavender) honey · ¾ cup water
12 green cardamom pods, lightly crushed**

In a saucepan over medium heat, combine the honey and water and warm, stirring to dissolve the honey, until just below the boiling point. Remove from the heat and stir in the cardamom pods. Cover and let stand at room temperature for 48 hours. Strain into a glass jar, cover, and refrigerate until needed. Makes about 1¼ cups.

basil syrup

1 cup sugar · 1 cup water · ½ cup loosely packed fresh basil leaves

In a saucepan over medium heat, combine the sugar and water and bring to a boil, stirring until the sugar is dissolved. Add the basil leaves and simmer for 5 minutes. Remove from the heat, cover, and let stand at room temperature for 8 hours. Strain into a glass jar, cover, and refrigerate until needed. Makes about 1½ cups.

ginger-lime syrup

2 cups cane syrup · One 3-inch piece fresh ginger, peeled and sliced · Finely grated zest from 4 limes

Pour the cane syrup into a saucepan over medium heat and warm until just below the boiling point. Remove from the heat and stir in the ginger and lime zest. Cover and let stand at room temperature for at least 1 hour, or preferably overnight (for greater intensity of flavor). Strain into a glass jar, cover, and refrigerate until needed. Makes about 1½ cups.

lemon thyme syrup

1 cup sugar · 1 cup water · 1½ tablespoons fresh lemon thyme leaves

In a saucepan over medium-high heat, combine the sugar and water and bring to a boil, stirring until the sugar is dissolved. Remove from the heat and stir in the lemon thyme leaves. Alternatively, to make **Thyme Simple Syrup**, use fresh regular thyme leaves. Cover and let stand at room temperature for at least 10 minutes or up to 1 hour. Strain into a glass jar, cover, and refrigerate until needed. Makes about 1½ cups.

lemon syrup

1 cup sugar · 1 cup water · Finely grated zest from 4 lemons

In a saucepan over medium-high heat, combine the sugar, water, and lemon zest and bring to a boil, stirring until the sugar is dissolved. Remove from the heat and let cool slightly. Strain into a glass jar and let cool completely. Cover and refrigerate until needed. Makes about 1½ cups.

salt & sugar rims

Rimming salts and sugars not only add visual appeal to a drink, but they can also improve its overall taste and provide another layer of flavor. Each of these rimming recipes makes about 3–4 tablespoons, enough to rim 4–6 glasses.

As in cooking, salt and sugar help balance and/or emphasize the ingredients in a cocktail. A spicy celery salt balances the acidity in a Bloody Mary while introducing complementary flavors. And a cinnamon-sugar rim can add depth to a cocktail featuring apple brandy or fruit purée. For an ethereal presentation, dust a crystal martini glass with a combination of superfine sugar and finely ground lemon zest.

lime salt

6 limes • 1 tablespoon Maldon or other coarse salt • 1 tablespoon superfine sugar

Preheat the oven to 200°F. Line a baking sheet with parchment paper. Using a rasp-style grater, finely grate the zest from the limes onto the prepared sheet. Bake until no moisture remains in the zest, 2–4 hours. Grind the zest to a powder in a spice grinder or clean coffee grinder. Sift through a fine-mesh sieve and measure the powder; you should have about 1 tablespoon. Place in a small bowl and stir in the salt and sugar until well combined.

celery salt

3 cups celery leaves • 1 teaspoon Blue Smoke Magic Dust or ¼ teaspoon cayenne pepper • 1 teaspoon Maldon or other coarse salt

Preheat the oven to 200°F. Line a baking sheet with parchment paper. Spread the celery leaves on the sheet. Bake until no moisture remains in the leaves, 2–4 hours. Grind the leaves to a powder in a spice grinder or clean coffee grinder. Sift through a fine-mesh sieve and measure the powder; you should have about 3 tablespoons. Place in a small bowl and stir in the Magic Dust and salt until well combined.

cilantro-lime salt

4 limes • 3 cups cilantro leaves • 1 tablespoon superfine sugar 1 teaspoon Maldon or other coarse salt

Preheat the oven to 200°F. Line 2 baking sheets with parchment paper. Using a rasp-style grater, finely grate the zest from the limes onto 1 of the prepared baking sheets. Spread the cilantro leaves on the other baking sheet. Bake until no moisture remains in the zest and leaves, 2–4 hours. Grind the zest to a powder in a spice grinder or clean coffee grinder. Sift through a fine-mesh sieve and measure the powder; you should have about 2 teaspoons. Repeat this step with the cilantro leaves; you should have about 2 tablespoons. Place the lime and cilantro powders in a small bowl and stir in the sugar and salt until well combined.

maple-vanilla-orange sugar

1 orange · 1 tablespoon turbinado sugar · 2 tablespoons granulated maple sugar · ⅜ teaspoon vanilla powder such as Nielsen-Massey · ⅛ teaspoon freshly ground allspice

Preheat the oven to 200°F. Line a baking sheet with parchment paper. Using a rasp-style grater, finely grate the zest from the orange onto the prepared sheet. Bake until no moisture remains in the zest, 2–4 hours. Grind the zest to a powder in a spice grinder or clean coffee grinder. Sift through a fine-mesh sieve and measure the powder; you should have about ¾ teaspoon. Place in a small bowl and stir in the sugars, vanilla powder, and allspice until well combined.

orange sugar

2 oranges · 2 tablespoons turbinado sugar · 2 teaspoons firmly packed light muscovado sugar (unrefined brown sugar), such as India Tree

Preheat the oven to 200°F. Line a baking sheet with parchment paper. Using a rasp-style grater, finely grate the zest from the oranges onto the prepared sheet. Bake until no moisture remains in the zest, 2–4 hours. Grind the zest to a powder in a spice grinder or clean coffee grinder. Sift through a fine-mesh sieve and measure the powder; you should have about 1½ teaspoons. Place in a small bowl and stir in the sugars until well combined.

lemon dust

6 lemons · 2 tablespoons superfine sugar

Set the oven to its lowest temperature (125°–150°F). Line a baking sheet with parchment paper. Using a rasp-style grater, finely grate the zest from the lemons onto the prepared sheet. Bake until no moisture remains in the zest, about 45–60 minutes. Do not let the lemon zest burn or have any brown coloring. Grind the zest to a powder in a spice grinder or clean coffee grinder. Sift through a fine-mesh sieve and measure the powder; you should have about 1 tablespoon. Place in a small bowl and stir in the sugar until well combined.

cinnamon sugar

¼ cup turbinado sugar · ½ teaspoon ground cinnamon

In a spice grinder or clean coffee grinder, combine the sugar and ground cinnamon. Pulse just to combine; the sugar should remain granular.

rimming a glass

To rim a glass with salt or sugar, fill a small plate that is wider than the rim of the glass with a shallow pool of the desired coating ingredient. Moisten the outside edge of the glass with a wedge of citrus, liqueur, simple syrup, or water. Holding the glass rim down at an angle, slowly rotate the outside edge through the coating ingredient to cover about ⅛-¼ inch of the rim, taking care not to get the coating inside the glass. Gently shake off any excess and use a moist towel to "clean" the edge to create a straight line.

fruit purées

Combine a fruit purée with a simple syrup (pages 214–215) to create inventive cocktails, or partner with a rimming salt or sugar (pages 216–217) for added complexity. Fruit purées will keep, tightly covered in the refrigerator, for up to 2 days, or in an ice cube tray in the freezer for up to 4 months.

If you don't have the time or the equipment to make purées at home, you can also purchase them. Look for brands La Fruitière and Perfect Purée online or at specialty-food stores like Dean & DeLuca. Goya fruit purées can be found in some grocery stores and Latin markets.

watermelon purée

1½ cups cubed watermelon • 1 tablespoon Simple Syrup (page 214), or to taste • ¼ teaspoon fresh lemon juice, or to taste

In a blender or food processor, combine the watermelon cubes, simple syrup, and lemon juice and purée until smooth. Taste and adjust the simple syrup and lemon juice as needed. Makes about 1 cup.

strawberry purée

1 cup fresh hulled strawberries • 2 tablespoons Simple Syrup (page 214), or to taste • ¼ teaspoon fresh lemon juice (optional)

In a blender or food processor, combine the strawberries and simple syrup and purée until smooth. Taste and adjust the simple syrup as needed or add lemon juice, if desired. Strain through a fine-mesh sieve. Makes about ½ cup.

passion fruit purée

10–15 fresh passion fruits • ¼ cup superfine sugar, or as needed

Set a small fine-mesh strainer over a glass measuring cup. Cut the passion fruit in half and scoop the yellow pulp and seeds into the strainer, discarding the rinds. Push the liquid through the strainer with the back of a spoon; discard the seeds. When you have just over ½ cup passion fruit pulp, stir in the sugar until dissolved. Taste and adjust the sugar as needed. Makes about ¾ cup.

blood orange purée

4 blood oranges, peeled, segmented, and seeded • 1 tablespoon Simple Syrup (page 214), or to taste • 1 teaspoon fresh lemon juice, or to taste

In a blender or food processor, combine the orange segments, simple syrup, and lemon juice and purée until smooth. Taste and adjust the simple syrup and lemon juice as needed. Makes about ¾ cup.

elegant garnishes

These fruit garnishes can add elegance and flavor to many cocktails. Passion Fruit Gelée Cubes contrast with dark chocolate in the Heart of Darkness (page 131); Drunken Cranberries spice up the Cranberry Daiquiri (page 73) and Winter Mojito (page 166); and Brandied Cherries add a kick to the Cherry Blossom Sling (page 67).

passion fruit gelée cubes

1 tablespoon unflavored powdered gelatin • ¼ cup water • ¾ cup superfine sugar, plus more for dusting • 1 teaspoon light corn syrup • ½ cup Passion Fruit Purée, homemade (page 218) or purchased

Oil an 8-by-5-inch loaf pan.

In a saucepan, sprinkle the gelatin over the water and let stand until softened, about 10 minutes. Stir in the sugar and corn syrup and place over medium-low heat. Stir until the sugar is dissolved, then raise the heat to medium-high and bring to a boil. Boil, swirling the pan occasionally, until the mixture is foamy and thick, 8–10 minutes; lower the heat if the mixture threatens to boil over or brown at the edges.

Remove from the heat, let the bubbles dissipate, and stir in the passion fruit purée. Pour through a fine-mesh sieve into the prepared loaf pan. Cover and chill until firmly set, 8–12 hours or up to 1 week.

Unmold onto a cutting board, trim the edges, and cut into small cubes. Pour the superfine sugar onto a plate, roll the gelées in the sugar, and serve. Makes about 60 gelées.

drunken cranberries

1½ cups Simple Syrup (page 214) • 2 cinnamon sticks • Zest from 1 large orange • 1 cup fresh cranberries • 1½ cups white rum, preferably Bacardi Silver

In a large saucepan, combine the simple syrup, cinnamon sticks, and the orange zest. Bring just to a boil over medium-high heat and add the cranberries. Cook until the cranberries just begin to pop and their skins begin to split, about 1 minute. Remove from the heat and let cool slightly, then strain the liquid into a large glass jar. Add the cranberries to the jar (discarding the cinnamon and orange zest), then add the rum. If the cranberries are not fully submerged in the liquid, add equal parts simple syrup and rum until they are completely covered. Let cool, then cover and refrigerate for at least 2 hours or up to 3 weeks. Makes about 3 cups.

brandied cherries

½ cup sugar • ½ cup water • 2 tablespoons fresh lemon juice 3 vanilla beans • 2 cinnamon sticks • 4 whole star anise pods 1 tablespoon whole cloves • 3 lb Bing cherries, pitted 5 tablespoons brandy, preferably Germain-Robin VSOP

In a large saucepan, combine the sugar, water, lemon juice, vanilla beans, cinnamon sticks, star anise, and cloves. Bring to a boil over medium-high heat, then reduce the heat to a simmer. Add the cherries and simmer until hot, 2–3 minutes. Remove from the heat and stir in the brandy. Let cool, then refrigerate for 8–12 hours. Strain the juice into a clean glass jar and add the cherries, discarding everything else. Tightly cover and refrigerate for up to 1 month. Makes about 4 cups.

spirits lexicon

A guide to many of the uncommon spirits and ingredients found in this book's recipes. Look for them online or at well-stocked liquor stores and specialty-beverage markets.

Absinthe
An anise-flavored spirit banned in many nations in the early 1900s (the bans have now been lifted in nearly every country).

Agave nectar
A natural, fructose-based sweetener made in Mexico from the juice extracted from the core of an agave plant.

Aperol
A bitter Italian aperitif, similar to and owned by Campari.

Applejack
A blend of distilled cider and neutral spirits produced in the United States.

Buddha's Hand Citron
A perfumed, lemon-like South Asian citrus fruit used in an infused vodka produced by Hangar One distillery in California.

Cachaça
A potent Brazilian spirit distilled from fresh sugarcane juice.

Carpano Antica
An Italian sweet vermouth that is smooth and full-bodied.

Chartreuse
An herbal liqueur produced by French monks; the yellow variety is milder than the green.

Cherry Heering
A deep red, Danish cherry liqueur.

Ginger beer
A slightly alcoholic, carbonated drink, flavored primarily with ginger, lemon, and sugar.

Gosling's Black Seal Rum
A dark rum with a rich, molasses-like flavor. It is mixed with ginger beer to create the Dark & Stormy (Bermuda's national drink).

Grappa
An Italian brandy made by distilling pomace, grape residue left over from winemaking.

Lillet
A French brand of aperitif made from Bordeaux wine fortified with Armagnac and a proprietary blend of herbs, spices, and fruit. Available in *blanc* (white) and *rouge* (red).

Maraschino liqueur
A clear, dry Italian liqueur distilled from crushed Dalmatian Marasca cherries, pits and stems included.

Mezcal
A spirit made in Mexico from the agave plant (whereas tequila production is limited to one variety of blue agave). Its smoky flavor comes from roasting the agave before fermentation.

Moscato d'Asti
A sweet, semi-sparkling wine produced in the Piemonte region of Italy from Moscato grapes.

Passoã
A brand of passion fruit liqueur sold in a signature black bottle.

Pernod
An anise-flavored absinthe substitute made by the French company that produced true absinthe before France banned it in 1914.

Pimm's No. 1
A gin-based drink—created by Londoner James Pimm—flavored with fruits and herbs.

Pisco
A clear South American spirit distilled from Muscat grapes.

Pommeau
An aperitif spirit made in northern France by mixing apple juice with apple brandy.

Prosecco
An aromatic, light sparkling wine produced in northeastern Italy.

Punt e Mes
An Italian sweet vermouth with a dark brown color and bitter flavor.

Rhum agricole
A type of rum from the French West Indies made from sugarcane juice; the Appellation d'Origine Contrôlée seal denotes high quality.

St-Germain
A French liqueur made from handpicked elderflower blossoms.

Underberg bitters
A proprietary brand of digestif bitters made in Germany. Other more commonly used bitters include Angostura (from Venezuela), Peychaud's (from New Orleans), and orange (produced by Regan's or Fee Brothers).

Velvet Falernum
A sugarcane-based liqueur with infusions of clove, almond, and lime, created in Barbados in the late 1800s.

bar tools

The following essential bar tools are detailed on page 14:

juicer	bar spoon
jigger	shaker
muddler	strainer

Below is a list of additional tools recommended for the home bar.

bar towels
Small, absorbent terry cloth towels keep hands dry, aid in cleaning up spills, and facilitate hand-crushing ice; lint-free smooth towels are best for polishing glassware. Be sure to have a ready supply of each.

channel knife
A commonly used small peeler with a metal tooth used for making long, thin citrus twists. Best used for small garnishes. If capturing the essential oils of the peel is desired, a vegetable peeler is the better choice.

citrus zester
Used to finely grate citrus peel. Look for a handheld microplane or rasp-style grater that is specifically designed for zesting citrus.

cocktail picks
Whether you prefer 4-inch bamboo skewers, stainless-steel skewers, or plastic picks, have some on hand to spear olives or onions, and to create more elaborate garnishes.

glassware
The importance of glassware cannot be overlooked. The fuller your collection, the more diverse a selection of cocktails you can serve and enjoy. Recommended basic glassware: 4 Collins glasses, 4 martini glasses, 4 old-fashioned glasses, 4 Champagne flutes, 2 snifters, and 2 hot toddy glasses.

ice molds
Silicone ice molds are available for cubes of all sizes. Those that make 1-by-1-inch cubes are the most versatile. Larger, silicone muffin molds or half-loaf molds are great for serving stronger drinks. Recommended: Silicone Zone.

ice scoop
A perforated version of this metal tool is especially useful when scooping ice from a large bowl as it allows for any melted ice to be drained away. Recommended: Drain Ice Scoop.

measuring cup
A measuring tool essential for making simple syrups or larger batches of drinks. Recommended: Oxo Angled Measuring Cup.

pour spout
A metal or plastic spout that fits into the neck of a bottle to facilitate easy and controlled pouring. Look for one with a narrow opening to allow for a slower pour.

service spoon
A long-handled spoon used to remove one garnish at a time without having to use your hands. A perforated version, which drains the liquid from the garnish, works best.

spice grater
Essential for garnishing drinks with fresh nutmeg or other spices. Look for a metal grater with a container to hold the spices.

straws
The basic plastic version is essential for creating delicious drinks. Have plenty on hand to taste-test cocktails before serving.

swizzle
A plastic, glass, or metal rod used for stirring. A stainless-steel iced tea straw is an ideal version as it also allows for sipping. Recommended: Bodum Straw Spoon.

utility knife and cutting board
Used to prepare fruits and other fresh cocktail ingredients and garnishes. A chef's knife and a paring knife will also prove useful.

vegetable peeler
An indispensable tool for removing the peel from citrus fruits for cocktail garnishes. Recommended: Oxo Good Grip Peeler.

waiter's corkscrew
Bartenders prefer this corkscrew because it is small and efficient. Look for one that has a double-hinged lever and a bottle opener for glass bottles. Recommended: Pulltap's Waiter's Corkscrew.

conversion chart

¼ fl oz = 1½ teaspoons
½ fl oz = 1 tablespoon
¾ fl oz = 1½ tablespoons
1 fl oz = 2 tablespoons
2 fl oz = ¼ cup
3 fl oz = ¼ cup + 2 tablespoons
4 fl oz = ½ cup
6 fl oz = ¾ cup
8 fl oz = 1 cup
12 fl oz = 1½ cups
16 fl oz = 2 cups = 1 pint
24 fl oz = 3 cups
32 fl oz = 4 cups = 1 quart
128 fl oz = 4 quarts = 1 gallon

index

223

INDEX

GOLD STREET PRESS

An imprint of Weldon Owen Inc.

MIXSHAKESTIR

Conceived and produced by Weldon Owen Inc.

415 Jackson Street, San Francisco, CA 94111

Telephone: 415 291 0100   Fax: 415 291 8841

In collaboration with Union Square Hospitality Group
24 Union Square East, New York, NY 10003

A WELDON OWEN PRODUCTION

Copyright © 2008 Weldon Owen Inc.
All rights reserved, including the right of reproduction
in whole or in part in any form.

The following recipes are adapted from
One Spice, Two Spice
by Floyd Cardoz with Jane Daniels Lear:
Warm Tomato Chutney (page 204)
Goan Guacamole (page 205)
Copyright © 2006 by
Floyd Cardoz with Jane Daniels Lear
Reprinted by permission of HarperCollins Publishers

The following recipes are adapted from
The Union Square Cafe Cookbook
by Danny Meyer and Michael Romano:
Roman-Style Marinated Olives (page 199)
Hot Garlic Potato Chips (page 203)
Bar Nuts (page 193)
Copyright © 1994 by
Danny Meyer and Michael Romano
Reprinted by permission of HarperCollins Publishers

First printed in 2008
Printed in China

Printed by SNP-Leefung
10 9 8 7 6 5 4 3 2 1
Library of Congress Cataloging-in-Publication
data is available.

ISBN 13: 978-1-934533-13-0
ISBN 10: 1-934533-13-0

WELDON OWEN INC.

Executive Chairman, Weldon Owen Group John Owen
CEO and President, Weldon Owen Inc. Terry Newell
Senior VP, International Sales Stuart Laurence
VP, Sales and New Business Development Amy Kaneko
Director of Finance Mark Perrigo
VP and Publisher Hannah Rahill
VP and Creative Director Gaye Allen
Associate Publisher Amy Marr
Editorial Assistant Julia Nelson
Senior Art Director Emma Boys
Designer and Illustrator Diana Heom
Production Director Chris Hemesath
Production Manager Michelle Duggan
Color Manager Teri Bell

ACKNOWLEDGMENTS

Weldon Owen wishes to thank the following individuals at Union
Square Hospitality Group: Karen Kochevar for project management
and editorial guidance; Ehren Ashkenazi, Jay Doran, Kevin Garry,
Omri Green, Sam Lipp, Stephen Mancini, Chris Murray, and Tyler
Vaughan for sharing their knowledge, talent, and creativity in the
bar; Kenny Callaghan, Floyd Cardoz, Robb Garceau, Rob Hirdt, Daniel
Humm, Gabriel Kreuther, and Nancy Olson for creating delicious
bar fare; Stephan Baroni, Terry Coughlin, Graceanne Jordan, Kevin
Mahan, Mark Maynard-Parisi, Christopher Russell, Jon Vandegrift,
and Tracy Wilson for running inspiring restaurants; and Danny Meyer,
Paul Bolles-Beaven, Richard Coraine, Michael Romano, and David
Swinghamer for leading this talented team.

We gratefully acknowledge editorial assistance from Lisa Atwood,
Heather Belt, Carrie Bradley, Ken DellaPenta, Kathryn Shedrick,
Sharon Silva, and Kate Washington. We would also like to thank
Richard Vassilatos for assistance with photography, Bernardo Gómez
Pimienta for glassware, and Marisa Zafran at the Parker Meridien.

All photography by Jim Franco except for the following:
Quentin Bacon (page 6, right center); Emma Boys (pages 4, upper
left; 5, lower right; and 184–185, center); Mark Jordan (page 8);
Lucy Schaeffer (page 187, right center)

Art reprinted courtesy of the artists:
Thomas Demand (*Clearing II*, end papers); Stephan Hannock (*Flooded
River for Dante and Hallie*, end papers; *New York Nocturne for
Jesse: Madison Square Park South*, pages 118–119); Robert Kushner
(*Cornucopia* and *Welcome*, end papers); Richard M. Polsky (*Watercolor
on Paper*, end papers, page 21, and back jacket)

UNION SQUARE HOSPITALITY GROUP
ushgnyc.com

UNION SQUARE CAFE
21 East 16th Street, NYC
212 243 4020
unionsquarecafe.com

GRAMERCY TAVERN
42 East 20th Street, NYC
212 477 0777
gramercytavern.com

ELEVEN MADISON PARK
11 Madison Avenue, NYC
212 889 0905
elevenmadisonpark.com

TABLA
11 Madison Avenue, NYC
212 889 0667
tablany.com

BLUE SMOKE & JAZZ STANDARD
116 East 27th Street, NYC
212 447 7733
bluesmoke.com

SHAKE SHACK
Madison Square Park,
Southeast Corner, NYC
212 889 6600
shakeshack.com

THE MODERN
The Museum of Modern Art
9 West 53rd Street, NYC
212 333 1220
themodernnyc.com

CAFE 2 AND TERRACE 5
The Museum of Modern Art
9 West 53rd Street, NYC
momacafes.com

HUDSON YARDS CATERING
640 West 28th Street, NYC
212 488 1500
hycnyc.com